GENDER AND SOCIAL THEORY

THEORIZING **SOCIETY**
Series editor: Larry Ray

Published titles
Mary Evans: *Gender and Social Theory*
Barry Smart: *Economy, Culture and Society*

GENDER AND SOCIAL THEORY

Mary Evans

Open University Press
Buckingham · Philadelphia

Open University Press
Celtic Court
22 Ballmoor
Buckingham
MK18 1XW

email: enquiries@openup.co.uk
world wide web: www.openup.co.uk

and
325 Chestnut Street
Philadelphia, PA 19106, USA

First Published 2003

A catalogue record of this book is available from the British Library

ISBN   0 335 20864 9 (pbk)   0 335 20865 7 (hbk)

Library of Congress Cataloging-in-Publication Data
Evans, Mary, 1946–
    Gender and social theory / Mary Evans.
        p. cm. – (Theorizing society)
    Includes bibliographical references and index.
    ISBN 0-335-20865-7 – ISBN 0-335-20864-9 (pbk.)
    1. Sex role–Sociological aspects. I. Title. II. Series.

HQ1075 .E928 2003
305.3–dc21   2002074969

Typeset by Graphicraft Limited, Hong Kong
Printed in Great Britain by Biddles Limited, Guildford and King's Lynn

CONTENTS

SERIES EDITOR'S FOREWORD

Sociology is reflexively engaged with the object of its study, society. In the wake of the rapid and profound social changes of the later twentieth century, it is important to question whether our theoretical frames of reference are appropriate for these novel configurations of culture, economy and society. Sociologists further need to ask whether recent theoretical preoccupations – for example with the 'cultural turn', post-modernism, deconstruction, globalization and identity adequately grasp social processes in the Millennium. One central issue here is the relationship between contemporary social problems and theories on the one hand and the classical heritage of Marx, Durkheim, Weber and Simmel on the other. Sociology is still reluctant to forget its founders and the relevance of the classical tradition is both powerful and problematic. It is powerful because the classics constitute a rich source of insights, concepts and analyses that can be deployed and reinterpreted to grasp current problems. But it is problematic because the social world of the classics is largely that of industrial, imperial and high bourgeois European societies prior to the First World War. How do we begin to relate the concepts formed in this milieu to the concerns of the globalized social world that is post-colonial, post-industrial and has seen the rise and collapse of Soviet socialism? Gender relations has been the site of one of the major transformations of the later twentieth century. While it would not be true to say that classical theory ignored issues of gender; it did presuppose a social world in which relations were highly gendered and to some extent at least inscribed within 'nature'. How does sociology reconfigure the relations between gender, identity and 'nature' in ways that disrupt attempts to naturalize social difference, yet avoid simplistic polarization? These are some of the major challenges for sociology that this series, Theorizing Society, aims to address.

This series intends to map out the ways in which social theory is being transformed and how contemporary issues have emerged. Each book in the series offers a concise and up-to-date overview of the principle ideas, innovations and theoretical concepts in relation to its topic. The series is designed to provide a review of recent developments in social theory, offering a comprehensive collection of introductions to major theoretical issues. The focus of individual books is organized around topics which reflect the major areas of teaching and research in contemporary social theory, including modernity, post-modernism, structuralism and post-structuralism; cultural theory; globalization; feminism and sexuality; memory, identity and social solidarity. While being accessible to undergraduates these books allow authors to develop personal and programmatic statements about the state and future development of theoretically defined fields.

In *Gender and Social Theory* Mary Evans explores the extent to which social theory has engaged with and illuminated the question of relations between genders and between gender and the social world. She aims to offer an account of the relationship between social theory and gender which both asks why gender matters to social theory and how sociological theory addresses the meaning and experience of gender? Evans further considers the way the issue of gender might disturb some of the traditional assumptions of social theory. Her approach is interdisciplinary, offering an understanding of sociology that resists confinement within a narrow disciplinary canon and the received tradition of classical theory. On the contrary, Evans explores the possibility of thinking about the range and contents of sociology, particularly through engagement with a diverse range of literature, including George Eliot, Malcolm Bradbury, Mary Shelley and Virginia Woolf, and making explicit the social theory implicit in these texts.

Gender and Social Theory maintains engagement with the 'founding fathers', especially Simmel, whose sociology opens up delicate, invisible threads that are woven between one person and another and an interrogation of the boundaries between the social and individual. An extensive discussion of Marx and Engels is interwoven with analysis of social theory in the nineteenth century novel. However, sociology no longer needs to genuflect at the feet of the classics, who assumed that most differences between men and women were 'natural'. This was a failure of the sociological imagination that, with more reflection, might have led the Grand Old Men of sociology to understand how all categories of difference are socially constructed and infused with relations of power.

Evans' analysis is informed by the 'cultural turn' in the social sciences, which she argues has opened themes of diversity, subjectivity, psychic and emotional life while weakening the disciplinary boundaries of sociology. Echoing Marshall Berman's famous quote from Marx, she argues that what was assumed to be solid in social life (e.g. economy) has 'turned to air' and lost theoretical space to culture. Along with this has developed a powerful sense of the contingency of existing social forms and the possibility of their transformation. Sensitivity to the cultural construction of social life is important to understanding the lived experience of the social world, gender and class. The shift from the politics of redistribution to recognition, along with acknowledging forms of domination that are inscribed into cultural practices, have been central to the critique of patriarchy and testify to the lasting impact of feminist theory. However, Evans does not suggest that culture has replaced all 'material' considerations and forms of oppression. On the contrary, production and productive relations remain is as important as ever and class continues to exert powerful influence on the structuration of gender divisions.

Throughout this volume Evans maintains dialectic interaction between the representation of gender in social theory and the impact of contemporary social changes on both feminism and social theory. With the end of industrial society comes the prospect of a 'crisis of masculinity' as the traditional markers of male identity – physical prowess, regular waged manual work, being a 'provider' – disappear with the vanishing working class communities that were once an important topic for sociological enquiry. The entry of women into the labour market (albeit on terms unequal with men) has increased the significance of paid employment as a site for understanding the dynamics of gender and (as Engels predicted) has contributed to the erosion of patriarchy. At the same, the transformation of intimacy and what Giddens calls the 'democratization' of gender relations has increase attention to the 'private', in both everyday life and social theory. In the process, the universal subject of earlier social theory has given way to increased awareness of difference.

Has feminist theory transformed social theory? One of its goals, to make women visible within the academy, has been achieved. It has further firmly placed women and gender on the sociological agenda. It is now impossible to study society without at the same time studying how society is constructed through male and female, masculinity and femininity. The concept of the gendered self has made a major contribution to debates about women, power and agency. However, Evans repeatedly reminds us of the complexity of gender issues and their relationship with structures of class and 'race'. Some theorists, such as Judith Butler maintain that there is no 'male' and 'female' person on whom scripts of sexually appropriate behaviour are imposed. However, Evans concludes that we cannot yet be human without gender identity but we cannot fulfil our humanity without recognition of the limitations and strengths of that identity. This is an important book that promises to refocus debates in both gender and social theory.

Larry Ray
Professor of Sociology
University of Kent

ACKNOWLEDGEMENTS

I am extremely grateful to Carole Phillips for her endlessly helpful contribution to the preparation of this manuscript. Her work, and interest in the project, have been invaluable. I should also like to thank Larry Ray for suggesting that I write this book, and for his helpful and characteristically generous and constructive comments. Matthew Taylor and Karl Thompson have provided considerable assistance, and Kate Reed and Janet Sayers were supportive readers. David, Tom and James Morgan have all contributed their individual understanding of the issues raised here and provided constant delight and joy in doing so.

INTRODUCTION

But the Vicar of St Botolph's had certainly escaped the slightest
tincture of the Pharisee, and by dint of admitting to himself that he
was too much as other men were, he had become remarkably unlike
them . . .

(George Eliot, *Middlemarch*)

If you ask them what is the meaning of their restless activity, why
they are never satisfied with what they have, thus appearing so
senseless to any purely worldly view of life, they would perhaps give
the answer, if they know any at all: 'to provide for my children and
grandchildren'. But more often, and since that motive is not peculiar
to them, but was just as effective for the traditionalist, more
correctly, simply: that business with its continuous work has
become a necessary part of their lives.

(Max Weber, *The Protestant Ethic & the Spirit of Capitalism*)

What can be said at all, can be said clearly.

(Wittgenstein)

The quotations above are intended to give readers an early indication of
some of the views and inclinations which inform this book. The first is a
commitment to the idea of interdisciplinarity. Thus the quotation from
George Eliot, and the suggestion to her readers in 1871 that it is only when
we recognize what we share with others that we begin to understand ourselves. We spend much of our lives, as Eliot recognizes, preoccupied with
our singularity and our individuality. It is a major task of sociology to
enable us to understand the common circumstances of our existence. That
assumption may occasionally be of comfort to us, but as the quotation from
Weber reminds us, it may also be unsettling and profoundly uncomfortable.
We may not want to recognize the part which we as individuals play in
structures of power and privilege: it is certainly not the case that we are
often prepared to recognize the elements of our behaviour which are
derived from the social as much as the personal world. But at the beginning
of the twenty-first century, when those of us who live in the West live in
societies of unparalleled technological sophistication (in particular in terms
of our ability to control and reorder the natural world) we increasingly,

and urgently, need to recognize that the needs, desires and inclinations which we assume to be 'natural' are part of a socially created world. We do not have to give paid work an absolute priority, we do not have to have certain consumer goods and we are not naturally entitled to follow wherever the 'pursuit of happiness' might lead us. These – and other assumptions about life in the West in the twenty-first century – are created by social processes and social structures.

The purpose of this book is to try and set out the extent to which social theory has engaged with and illuminated the question of relations between the genders and between gender and the social world. The book is not an account of the absence of gender in social and sociological theory. That question, at least in the most literal sense, has already been examined. It is rather an examination and a discussion of the ways in which the issue of gender might disturb or lead us to re-examine some of the traditional assumptions of social theory. But that re-examination, it must also be said, does not assume that there is such an easily identifiable area of knowledge known as 'social theory'. There is an element of consensus about the main contributors to the classic tradition of sociology, but in these pages I also wish to raise the question that thinking about society and social relations has to involve subjects other than those of sociology. Thus, although the focus of this book is sociological literature, I have used the term 'social' theory to denote my interest in ideas and theoretical accounts from outside it. In part this view is now conventional enough, in that the widely documented 'cultural turn' in sociology has shifted thinking about the range and content of the subject. But I also wish to suggest that the cultural turn should be allowed to include the understanding of both culture and society given to us *by* aspects of our culture, notably the disciplines of literature and history. Hence readers will find that these pages include references to works of fiction, and fiction that is used as both example and as theory-in-itself.

Furthermore, this text is explicitly concerned with gender and the relations of gender. It is inevitable, therefore, that feminist writing (drawn from diverse disciplines) should figure large in these pages. Second-wave feminism has contributed both to our understanding *and* our experience of contemporary society. It is thus appropriate that a book which is concerned with the social should allow a significant presence to a *corpus* of writing which has radically disturbed many conventional expectations and assumptions about the social world. Feminism – in common with those other great narratives of Marxism and psychoanalysis – did not originate in the academy, but rather has been integrated into the academy and used (and some might well say abused) by it. But it is unquestionably part of 'society' in the twenty-first century and thus it appears here as both subject – a voice which must disturb the traditional order of gender – and object, a social movement which, like others, merits attention. However, the voice of this text is as informed by feminism as by other accounts of the social world and makes no attempt to chase 'objectivity' or the 'scientific'. What follows is presented as an argument about our theoretical understanding of the way in which we live in contemporary western society.

With a commitment to both interdisciplinarity and subjectivity goes a commitment to writing which can be easily understood and is not scattered with those technical terms and phrases which defeat many readers. 'Technologization' (an ugly word in itself) has become an aspect of our culture, but it seems to me that there is no justification for writing in a way which demands the endless use of a dictionary or a glossary of terms. Thus, alongside a recognition of the theoretical possibilities of disciplines other than sociology goes a determination to write as inclusively as possible. Finally, the purpose of this book is both to suggest ways in which sociology has considered gender (and illuminated our understanding of it) and to identify ways in which, as suggested, thinking about gender might enliven and enrich sociology.

CHAPTER I

ENTER WOMEN

In *Daniel Deronda*, George Eliot raises the question which is a problem for any writer, whether of fiction or non-fiction, of where to begin. My reference here to George Eliot and to nineteenth-century narrative fiction is also indicative of a theme which informs this discussion of gender and social theory – namely that although the academic world may find it appropriate to divide understanding and information in ways which correspond to academic disciplines, the lived world is less likely to impose boundaries on how we act in, think about and experience it. Thus we do not think 'politically' about politics, or 'sociologically' about the social world. We construct (and consult) accounts of what we do, and what we might do, but those accounts are informed as much by the everyday world as by academic accounts and discussions. In the pages that follow I do not, therefore, intend to interpret sociology, social theory or the sociological in the narrow terms of an academic discipline or its worst excesses of definition in a benchmarking document. What I wish to do is to acknowledge first of all the 'turn to culture' which has been defined (in particular by Michele Barrett) and articulated by other authors; and second, in relation to that first point, to confront the implications for social theory and what Barrett has described as the decimation of the claims of materialism.[1]

Materialism – usually in the form of more or less sophisticated interpretations of Marxism – dominated British sociology throughout the 1960s and 1970s. The 'turn to culture' (in part a consequence of the challenge to a Marxism which was blind to issues about gender and race) shifted the relationship of sociology and social theory to the study of modernity. While it was not quite the case that (in the words of Marshall Berman's book) *All That is Solid Melts into Air*, a great deal of what was assumed as the solid basis of sociology and social theory (the study of paid work and political economy for example) did lose theoretical space to the study of culture.[2]

Yet is was one of the great strengths of sociology that in contemporary western culture – a culture of rampant individualism – it asserted the existence of the general, shared, material context. But the weakness of sociology often lay in that strength – that in identifying the general, the individual (and in particular the individual and particular case which illuminates the general) is lost. Thus this book opens with a reference to one of the great English writers of the nineteenth century; an imaginative voice which matches in its understanding of the social world that of Marx or Weber, but which chose the realm of fiction rather than that of social reality through which to express it. Eliot's social theory is of course implicit rather than explicit, like that of social theorists. Nevertheless, a theory of the social world is clearly part of *Middlemarch* (just as there is a theory of class relations in Elizabeth Gaskell) and hence this book will attempt to provide not just an account of the relationship between gender and theory, but a more eclectic view of 'theory' than has generally been presented in the past by those who write about it. If the 'cultural turn' means anything, it must, I would argue, mean that as much as studying culture as an object, we also integrate the understandings offered to us by culture in our accounts of the social world.

It is apparent from the work of Vikki Bell (and other authors such as Dorothy Smith, Sylvia Walby, Jackie Stacey, Sarah Franklin and Celia Lury) that we need no longer interpret 'social theory' in terms of genuflection at the feet of Marx, Weber and Durkheim, or assume that sociology's concerns are only with the public space of the social world: the world of paid work, for example, or the political behaviour of specific groups.[3] One of the most widely read sociology texts of the past ten years has been Anthony Giddens' *The Transformation of Intimacy*, and others – for example, Stevi Jackson and Simon Williams – have examined what might once have been described as the private life of individuals.[4] I would argue that these accounts of psychic and emotional life at the end of the twentieth and the beginning of the twenty-first centuries are certainly significant, in that they illuminate those areas of life which are, for many people, the most important part of their existence, but that this concern with the psychic life of individuals has always been a part of sociology and social theory. We applaud Jackson, Duncan *et al.* for turning to the study of emotional life, but they are part of a tradition which includes Max Weber's great study of the impact of Protestantism on Europe in the sixteenth and seventeenth centuries.[5] This account of the remaking of the psychic life of Europe, a way of life which we still share and experience, needs to be remembered when claims are made about the previous refusal of sociology to involve itself in the study of the inner world of individuals.

By this point, readers will perhaps have some idea of my sympathies (and absence of sympathy). They are for the interdisciplinary, indeed multi-disciplinary, study of the social world and a review of the claims and achievements of the past. They are against an interpretation of sociology with narrowly defined boundaries and concerns, or assumptions that only recent or contemporary sociologists have claims to a gendered understanding of the social world. There is also another sympathy which needs voicing at this point: a sympathy for a view of the social world of the twenty-first century which emphasizes (although does not always prioritize) the centrality of the material and the economic in individual lives. This might be called Marxist were it not for the fact that this label is too evocative of accounts of the social world which are often too mechanistic to arouse much recognition – let alone sympathy – in many readers. Capitalism, and capitalist social relations, may be the cause of much human and social misery (indeed they are precisely this) but they are explanations which often minimize individual difference, choice and agency.

However, while we may wish to believe that we live in a post-Marxist world in which consumption is the crucial social role in which we engage, I would argue that production, and engagement in it, is still as important as it has ever been. We may suppose that 'I shop, therefore I am', but we cannot shop without money. Class, as Beverley Skeggs has so cogently and persuasively argued, is alive and well, and playing a central role in the determination of the experience of individual social life.[6] Thus, although the beginning of this chapter acknowledged the turn to culture, a qualification is introduced here which can be illustrated by reference to the work of Virginia Woolf.

Woolf attempted to develop, in both her fiction and her non-fiction, an aesthetic that would be both feminist and modernist. In ways which were often very similar to those of Georg Simmel, Joan Rivière and Walter Benjamin, she defined and explored the ways in which we construct our identities in that definitive location of modernity, the cosmopolitan city.[7] Yet Woolf, as her dairies, letters and *A Room of One's Own* attest, recognized the centrality of money and income to any possibility of women's meaningful participation in this world.[8] Woolf, Rivière and Benjamin all wrote in a world informed by Freud and psychoanalysis (indeed, Virginia and Leonard Woolf were instrumental in the translation into English of Freud's work) and this knowledge of the sources and the roots of both the imagination and the rational has inevitably posed problems for accounts of the social world which assume a simple model of causality. That great title by the psychoanalyst Marion Milner, *The Suppressed Madness of Sane Men* epitomizes those connections between the inner and outer world of the individual, and of groups of individuals, which now increasingly inform our understanding of the social world but also make it more difficult to assume explanations of social action and human agency which are limited to single causes.[9] However, unlike later cultural critics, Woolf, Simmel and Benjamin all acknowledged the context in which individuals experienced the world – a context which for all of them included an appreciation of the material as individually experienced.

In the chapters that follow I shall develop at greater length some of the themes indicated above. Before turning to that discussion, however, it is important to say something about the title, and the thesis, of this book. The word 'gender' is part of the title because what this book will attempt to do is to give an account of social theory in relation to questions about gender: first, what does social theory have to say about gender and the social organization of gender; second, how do theories about gender inform and/ or illuminate social theory; and third, what is the substance of the claims made that theories of gender make no difference to social theory or, conversely, destabilize it so completely that traditional social theory is rendered obsolete?

Before embarking on an account of the above, the question of the meaning and implications of the word 'gender' confronts us. There are numerous definitions of the word (of which one of the most widely used is that by Ann Oakley), but the hidden agenda of the word 'gender' is about the ownership of the literature related to the word.[10] 'Gender studies' and the study of 'gender' have now become taken-for-granted parts of the literature throughout the social sciences, but the elevation of gender to a term of as much importance as that of class or race owed a great deal to the emergence of academic feminism in the 1970s. Prior to this date, the study of gender difference and the specific study of women or men was not entirely absent from the social science curriculum, but it was very limited. Most limited of all (almost non-existent in fact) was the assumption in the study of gender that there was a generalized social oppression and exploitation of women. The word 'patriarchy' obviously existed before 1970, but it was academic feminism which gave the word its particular meaning of the power of all men over all women. While previous interpretations of the word might have emphasized the way in which it implied the authority of men over general populations (or old men over young men, as in the expression 'the rule of the patriarchs'), feminists used the word as the starting point for the study of women and their social subordination. Even when there was disagreement about the use of the term 'patriarchy' (in, for example, the exchanges between Sheila Rowbotham, Sally Alexander and Barbara Taylor) there was a consensus that women were generally less socially privileged than men.[11]

Throughout the 1970s and much of the 1980s, the word 'gender' belonged to feminism. Those university degrees and courses which were established in this period were generally (although not exclusively) labelled as degrees or courses in women's studies, in which the study of gender was a part. For various reasons, intellectual and political, the term 'women's studies' began to be replaced in the 1990s by the term 'gender studies': an indication that what was now recognized was the impossibility of the study of women without the study of men. The focus of the academic work in question remained that of gender difference, but the possibility was now entertained that the way in which gender was constructed had as much to do with men as with women. There is, as many individuals have pointed out, a neutralizing and de-politicizing element in the term 'gender studies' as opposed to that of 'women's studies'.[12] Most particularly, gender studies does not represent that specific claim to notice, definition and particularity which is implied in the term 'women's studies'. However, this book is not about women's studies or gender studies, but gender and social theory. In this context the use of the term 'gender' rather than 'women' (or 'feminism') is a deliberate recognition not of the claims of men against women, but of the impact of the social world on constructions of both masculinity and femininity. Theories and accounts of the social world are the focus here, rather than the experiences of one or other half of the population. Having said that, no account of contemporary social theory would be complete without some discussion of the emergence and impact of academic feminism.

In the past 30 years, second-wave feminism has systematically engaged with the academy and academic disciplines. First-wave feminism – the feminism of the nineteenth and early twentieth centuries – was committed to the integration of western women into dominant models of citizenship. Thus, to this era of feminism, issues such as the vote and access to education were crucial.[13] It was also, of course, the case that first-wave feminism existed at a time when the universities were the preserve of a small minority of white, middle-class men. The curriculum of the academy was simply not an issue for feminists at the beginning of the twentieth century, whose concerns were with entry to the universities rather than a renegotiation of the subject matter. But that was to change in the late twentieth century: the expansion of higher education in the West – essentially a phenomenon of all western societies – coincided with the re-emergence of a public, feminist voice. Feminism did not, as the terms 'first-' and 'second-' wave feminism might suggest, disappear in the period 1920–70, but it did not achieve mass public attention or notice. The politics of the period 1925–45 were the politics of the rise of European Fascism; the subsequent post-war world was essentially a time dominated by the project of the establishment of western models of political conservatism and domestication.

At the beginning of the twenty-first century we can look back on this period (1945–65) and identify much which demonstrated the fault lines of apparent domestic tranquillity. Yet for many people in the West, the post-war years were years of tranquillity and prosperity. This peace (or illusion of peace) was shattered in the 1960s by a diversity of social movements and social changes. In the USA the protests, ongoing for decades, by black people about their civil status became more vocal and a national and international, rather than a localized, issue. Resistance to the escalation of involvement by the USA in Vietnam provided a politics which united people across countries. Moral and sexual certainties – or apparent *public* certainties – were challenged by the emergence of a youth culture made possible by a degree of affluence and a buoyant labour market. 'Sexual intercourse', wrote Philip Larkin, 'began in 1963'.[14]

These changes united in suggesting that the political, public world was far from stable and consensual, and was related in many ways to the private world of the domestic space. When Sylvia Plath, at the end of her life, wrote *The Bell Jar* (first published under a pseudonym in 1963), she articulated in fiction a set of links between the public and the private which were to become commonplace for later writers.[15] A feminist slogan of the 1970s was 'the personal is political', and it is precisely this understanding with which *The Bell Jar* opens. In the first chapter of the novel, Plath's heroine, Esther Greenwood, voices her horror at the execution of the Rosenbergs, accused of spying for the Soviet Union. Her next action is to voice her concerns about her own situation: as a successful student journalist she is being entertained and fêted in New York. Yet in this success, Plath/Greenwood can find only confusion and bafflement. How is she, as a woman, to be successful in a world which assumes that professional success for women is bizarre and at the best only to be tolerated? Equally, Plath/Greenwood look at the model of domestic life offered to her in the suburban USA and recognizes that it is a life organized around the double standard of sexual morality and a social division of labour which assigns women and children to the home and men to the public world. 'When I was nineteen,' says Plath's heroine, 'pureness was the great issue'. With the same knowing irony as Larkin, Plath lampooned the concern about the 'regulation' of sexuality when she wrote: 'Instead of the world being divided up into Catholics and Protestants or Republicans and Democrats or white men and black men or even men and women, I saw the world divided into people who had slept with somebody and people who hadn't'.[16]

Since 1963, and the publication of *The Bell Jar*, the western social world has, in many respects, changed. The suburbs and the sexual morality which so terrified and appalled Plath – and were equally appalling to Betty Friedan, whose *The Feminine Mystique* was published in the same year as *The Bell Jar* – still exist, but they have been radically disturbed by escalating rates of divorce and by economic factors which have made it difficult for the model of the one (male) breadwinner household to be sustained.[17] The domestic world, of which Plath and Friedan wrote, is no longer the same, even it if remains the ideal of conservative politicians throughout the West. The debates about 'latch-key' children, sexual permissiveness and 'working wives', all of which informed discussion of the 1960s, have disappeared as social reality, as much as ideological change has rendered them redundant.

It is a general assumption about the cultural history of the West that the 1960s were a decade of ideological transformation and rethinking. Indeed, 1968 is certainly regarded as the year in which the West, and France in particular, was brought within a hair's breadth of revolutionary change as a result of radical, and often spontaneous, politics. Certainly the 1960s saw the development of the sense of the possibility of social change and a recognition that social institutions, as much as being created by people, could also be overthrown by them. To historians, or anyone with even a limited knowledge of history, this was hardly surprising news. But to many people in the West this sense of the security of the post-1945 social world was such that these changes seemed both unique in human history and consequently terrifying. To be young in 1968 was perhaps not quite the 'bliss' that Wordsworth had suggested about 1789, but youth and social change were linked in ways which had profound implications for later cultural politics.

Sylvia Plath's response to the public and private politics of the Eisenhower years in the USA had been, both in fiction and in real life, an articulation of the mental and emotional turmoil which she, the individual, bore as a result of social complexity and contradiction. By the end of the 1960s this individual response to expectations about the role and position of women was no longer acceptable to a growing number of women. It was thus that at the beginning of the 1970s, rather than in the 1960s themselves, that a number of feminist books were published which argued that women were exploited and oppressed within western societies. Women's unhappiness and discontent was not, it was said, personal but structural. The list of feminist books published between 1970 and 1975 would fill several pages, but among those which made the most impact both at the time and subsequently were Shulamith Firestone's *The Dialectic of Sex*, Sheila Rowbotham's *Hidden from History*, Kate Millett's *Sexual Politics* and Germaine Greer's *The Female Eunuch*.[18] In retrospect, the differences between these authors is considerable and their subsequent development after the publication of these early books has demonstrated the extent of the difference. But at the time the books and their authors were seen as part of a shared protest at the situation of women in industrial societies, and at the absence of a public voice for women in political and institutional life. The social world of the late twentieth century was portrayed, in this literature, as a world which was misogynistic and exploitative of women. The literature and philosophy of the West was attacked as a history of male supremacy, while the social and institutional structures of both western, and state socialist societies, were seen as being organized in the interests of men. Firestone, Millett, Rowbotham and Greer were just a few of the feminist authors who, with anger and conviction, demanded a rethinking and restructuring of western (and indeed global) gender relations.

These – and other – powerful voices were to be the inspiration for a generation of young women who were, in the late 1960s and early 1970s, the members of the first generation of women to profit from the expansion of higher education. Until the 1970s, higher education in western Europe, although rather less so in the USA, had been the preserve of an élite (in 1965, approximately 6 per cent of 18-year-olds in the UK were in higher education). There was thus a coincidence in terms of the emergence of a coherent and visible feminist consciousness with a possible audience: the changed times of the 1960s and the sense of the possibility of the creation of a new culture appeared at the same time as increasing numbers of women entered the public worlds of the universities. What existed in those worlds, now seen through the lens of feminism, left much to be desired. Unlike the generation of women who were grudgingly admitted to higher education at the beginning of the twentieth century, the women who became under- graduates in the 1960s and 70s were empowered by a public endorsement of the social need for more graduates and an ideology which asserted the 'right' of individuals to higher education. In this new world, in which women were assumed to be just as much the legitimate beneficiaries of expanded higher education as men, it was inevitable that women would begin to ask questions about the nature and content of the academic world. What became clear to many women was the relative absence of women from the academic curriculum. Women – whether as authors or agents – were either not there or simply subsumed into the ungendered and inclusive term 'people', a term which was often assumed to be synonymous with men. The curriculum in subjects throughout the humanities and the social sciences assumed that the general human subject was a male, and often a white, middle-class male as well. The first-year course at the University of Sussex which was described as 'Plato to Nato' was seen, at its inception, as a bold exercise in interdisciplinarity. Ten years later it was seen as indicative of the unthinking assumption that the public world, and the world of ideas, was largely a world of men. By 1975 the exercise of correction, of which this book is part, had begun.

It is impossible to separate academic feminism from second-wave fem- inism since, both in terms of the individuals involved and the issues of the academic subset, there is considerable overlap. What is important, how- ever, is to note that – despite what has been said above – there was before the emergence of academic feminism in the West in the 1970s work by women, and men, in the academy which specifically identified women as the subject matter. Thus what I want to emphasize at the beginning of this study is that a division of the intellectual world into pre- and post-second- wave feminism overlooks the contribution of those writing before this period. The second point I would make here is that we should not be too literal-minded in our search for 'women' in the academic curriculum before 1970. Women, as a group, as a collectivity, may be relatively difficult to find, but the issue of gender difference and the nature of masculinity and femininity was a concern for some writers. A third and final point to make about the academic curriculum in general (and sociology is no exception here) is that in the main it has been set in the West. The West dominates academic debate and western universities maintain a dominant position in terms of the production of knowledge. Universities exist throughout the world, and there are local differences in terms of subject matter. But it is in the West that lie the universities and the academies whose work is the most widely known and the most generally distributed.

Social and sociological theory are part of this global culture as much as it has been formed, in the past 30 years, by feminist debates and concerns. As a subject, sociology was accused, like other conventional academic disciplines, of being blind to the concerns, ideas and situation of women. This charge is part of a more extensive discussion later in this chapter, but here I would argue that the charge is both exaggerated and inappropriate. More important here is the question of the history of sociology itself, and the complex relationship of the subject to modernity, the academy and social praxis. Students coming to sociology for the first time are generally introduced to the subject via the history of the great, canonical thinkers: Comte, Marx, Durkheim and Weber. These founding fathers were both theoreticians and (with the possible exception of Durkheim) individuals who were much concerned with the practical organization of society. Weber and Marx were both much involved in politics and neither could be accused of that 'ivory tower' isolation which is often attributed to contemporary academics. Their hands were much dirtied by contact with political life. In this they share an important characteristic with many feminist sociologists (and academics in general) whose work has been intensely involved with practical politics. As Martha Nussbawm has pointed out:

> For a long time, academic feminism has been closely allied to the practical struggle to achieve justice and equality for women. Feminist theory has been understood by theorists as not just fancy words on paper; theory is connected to proposals for social change. Thus feminist scholars have engaged in many concrete projects: the reform of rape law; winning attention and legal redress for the problems of domestic violence and sexual harassment; improving women's economic opportunities, working conditions, and education; winning pregnancy benefits for female workers; campaigning against the trafficking of women and girls in prostitution; working for the social and political equality of lesbians and gay men.[19]

These words were written to give some indication of the range of campaigns and concerns with which feminist academics (in this case largely in the social sciences) have been identified. A further characteristic of the account is that it suggests the *reforming* project of academic feminism, a project similar to that of the 'founding fathers' of sociology. In both contexts, and for both groups, knowing about society was the first step in the process of changing it. The degree of projected change obviously differed radically between Comte and Marx, but that degree of difference has been similarly shared by feminist academics. For Marxist feminists the project has remained – as the allegiance to Marxism implies – one of radical transformation, while for others the project is about more specific and more limited changes and reforms.

The purpose of this brief return to the 'founding fathers' is to raise the question of the relationship of theory to practice. This issue is one which has given rise to a considerable debate within feminism in terms of whether or not it is desirable that feminists should try and work within the academy.[20] But what is at least as important as the recognition of this debate is the recognition of and discussion about the relationship of the academy to the 'real' world. It is apparent that the many feminists who became academics (and academics who became feminists) in the 1970s saw the academy as a place in which individual work could contribute to general social change. The expectations of this view were, to a certain extent, fulfilled by such changes in social policy as shifts in ideas about rape in marriage or levels of financial provision to those individuals who care for others. Feminist academics in law, social policy, sociology and economics all made important contributions to changes in institutional arrangements. Yet at the same time as the academic groundwork was being prepared for these modifications in public policy, a continuing theme throughout the 1970s and 1980s was the general refusal of academic disciplines to consider women. Despite the fact that in most social science subjects there was a considerable record of academic engagement in the 'real' world, the criticism continued that the academy was remote and misogynist.

This is not the context in which to review the institutional practices of the academy. That within the academy there exists considerable prejudice against women (as in other professional contexts) is undeniable. But the form of prejudice which is important here is not that of institutional prejudice against either individual women or women as a group, but of prejudice in the discussion of women. The need to make this distinction is important because it enables us to do two things: to note the work by men which has considered women and to note the ways in which women doing academic work about women are the subjects of discriminatory judgements. In short, we need to try and distinguish, if possible, the subject matter and the individual. The importance of doing this is not just that it enables us to see exactly where prejudice lies, and at what and whom it is directed, but also because it enables us to escape from the theoretically limiting position which assumes that only work specifically about women is directly relevant to us.

At this point in the argument I think it is important to declare my own view of sociology – from where, as it is said, 'I am coming'. In my view, the term 'sociology' means a study of the processes and structures of the social world in a way originally outlined by Simmel in 1907:

> We can no longer take to be unimportant consideration of the
> delicate, invisible threads that are woven between one person

and another if we wish to grasp the web of society according to its productive, form-giving forces; hitherto, sociology has largely been concerned to describe this web only with regard to the finally created pattern of its highest manifest levels.[21]

The politics of sociology should therefore be an integration of the social and the individual: a recognition that the social world is formed by individual, social acts. Equally, when we study this world we have to recognize our own subjectivity. Thus I would argue that in sociology we must always ask *why* we want to know, quite as much as we have to ask about *what* we want to know. No social action or social process takes place in a social vacuum. We are all citizens of an industrial, capitalist world and although we act as individuals we are also individuals formed by general cultural and common experiences. Women and men are social actors and social beings. We are also people who share particular histories and identities: we may be women, but we are also middle- or working-class, Jewish or Catholic, heterosexual or homosexual. Hence, in these initial pages it is important to establish that the term 'woman' is problematic in terms of the degree of community with others which it assumes.

However, the title of this volume is not *Women and Sociological Theory*, but *Gender and Social Theory*. Thus, despite the focus above on feminism, I want to emphasize that the concerns discussed here are not just those of women but of women *and* men. To return to Sylvia Plath and *The Bell Jar*, and to the comments of Philip Larkin about the 1960s: both recognized the prisons of gender stereotyping for not one but for both sexes. Plath could identify, with ruthless accuracy, the limitations of the form of masculinity imposed upon western men in the 1950s, just as Larkin recognized the two sides of the apparently 'natural' domestic division of labour:

> Oh, no one can deny
> That Arnold is less selfish than I.
> He married a woman to stop her getting away
> Now she's there all day,
>
> And the money he gets for wasting his life on work
> She takes as her perk
> To pay for the kiddies' clobber and the drier
> And the electric fire,[22]

Larkin, as readers of Andrew Motion's biography will know, spent much of his life avoiding reproduction and domestic life. But in avoiding both, he voiced his recognition of the costs of conventional patterns of marriage and family life with just as much vehemence as Sylvia Plath. Both authors, widely read throughout the West, rebelled against domestic orthodoxy. 'They fuck you up, your mum and dad', growled Larkin, at much the same time as Sylvia Plath told 'Daddy' that she was 'through'. Approximately ten years later, Ann Oakley was to produce studies of housework and the lives of 'housewives' which gave a general account of women's experience of domestic life; but these accounts, vital and evocative as they are, do not match the passionate intensity of the rage of Larkin and Plath against the literal – and metaphysical – prisons of the conventionally established domestic worlds.[23]

Plath and Larkin provide the first example of what I hope to suggest in this volume – that sources other than those of the strictly sociological can illuminate, enhance and empower our understanding of both sociological theory and the relationship of the study of gender to it. But the use of these two authors, both well known and widely read throughout the English-speaking world, is also to suggest the two possible sides (of women and men) to a common social arrangement: that of heterosexual marriage and domestic life. Larkin and Plath, in their poetry, both suggest (albeit ambiguously) reservations about what sociologists describe as the domestic division of labour and the internal order of the household. Ann Oakley (in common with Hannah Gavron and other sociologists who have written about the family and gender relations within it) is inspired by a similar wish to challenge and question received opinions and conventional assumptions.[24] But the difference between her work and that of Larkin and Plath is that of the difference between the personal and the political. Oakley wished to demonstrate, through the tools of a particular discipline, shared reservations about a form of social arrangement. Larkin and Plath made no such claims to the general, but they articulated ideas which we can safely assume informed (if not directly then at least indirectly) the work of Oakley and others.

The point, therefore, is that as sociologists we are inspired by the culture in which we live. We read novels and poetry, we listen to music and we watch television. Then we study them. But in doing this we may do no more than illustrate and generalize what has already been suggested in the culture. The lens of the disenchantment with domestic life through which Plath and Larkin expressed their ideas was very powerful, as it was in the 1970s and 1980s for feminists who raged against the abuses of patriarchal power and authority. At the beginning of the twenty-first century there is correspondingly passionate concern to be found among those with concern for the environment. Sociology, however, is currently inspired by little vital political concern: feminism has achieved at least partial academic recognition and the nature of existing domestic arrangements in Britain and other industrialized countries suggests a considerable range of possibility, and certainly fewer expectations of the rigidly conventional, than in previous decades. If we accept the findings of sociologists such as Arlie Hochschild and Richard Scase, then the adult human being of the twenty-first century is one who prefers to live alone and prefers the life of work to that of the household.[25] Even if these arrangements create the sense of alienation and social deracination portrayed by Robert Putnam and Richard Sennett, we have to consider that the twenty-first century appears to have diminished differences of gender and to have emancipated both sexes from narrow expectations of particular gender 'roles'.[26]

It may, therefore, be the case that it is redundant to use the term 'gender' in sociology, in that the social world of the twenty-first century is actually that androgynous, bureaucratized world described by George Orwell in *Nineteen Eighty-Four*, and predicted at least in part as a 'polar night' by Max Weber.[27] It may equally be that gender no longer makes a defining difference to an individual's social experience, and that it only mattered for brief periods in the twentieth century when women were refused access to full participation in the public and social world. This suggestion will be seen as deeply heretical in many quarters (including those institutional contexts such as the Equal Opportunities Commission which are dedicated to the elimination of discrimination against women) but it is made not out of a belief in its veracity but to indicate a commitment to raising the question of examining the importance of gender in the social world. It has come to be accepted that gender 'matters' and, as with any orthodoxy, any idea which is generally accepted needs critical evaluation. This is not to suggest that we abandon the idea that gender plays a part in the structure of social organization. Everyday experience tells us that we have different expectations about the behaviour of women and men and these expectations are visible in any family, school or workplace. But the acceptance of this idea is very far from the account of the social world given by Pamela Abbott and Clare Wallace in their work, *An Introduction to Sociology: Feminist Perspectives*:

> Men and women, oppressors and oppressed, confront one another in their everyday lives – they are not just role-players acting out a prepared script. Human actors in specific social contexts can and do oppose each other; men do exercise power and women do experience pain and humiliation. However, the power of men over women is collective, society's sexist assumptions advantage all men – patriarchal ideologies support and sanction the power of men over women.[28]

This passage is followed by the statement that 'sociology needs feminism', and an argument is made which suggests that sociology has hitherto ignored women.

This discussion of gender and sociological theory does not attempt to demonstrate or invalidate that claim. What I intend to do here is to offer an account of the relationship of social theory and gender which asks why gender matters to sociological theory, and how sociological theory has – and might – discuss the meaning and experience of gender. Sociological theory is not static, but neither is the social world on which it depends for its subject matter. Nor does the social world change in relation to sociological theory. Thus we have to confront the issue of social change and social theory: sociology can describe the present, but it is more interesting when it attempts – as, for example, Weber attempted to do – to predict the future. Feminist agency, whether in politics generally or in sociological theory more particularly, has always tended to be reactive (i.e. a form of resistance to exclusions or discriminations) or protective (i.e. a defence of a specifically female space against masculine intrusion). So it has been with much feminist sociology: a protest about those issues related to women which are not discussed by men. The purpose of this book is not to continue in that mode, but to suggest ways in which thinking about gender (i.e. the discussion of the relationship between the sexes) can disturb sociological theory. The chapters that follow will not therefore be an account of what sociology (in the embodied form of male theorists) is supposed to have not said about gender (or more usually about women), but an account of the possibilities which thinking about gender offer to sociological and social theory.

Central to those possibilities are two ideas. The first is that in thinking about gender we have to think about an area of our lives which we can best describe as 'the personal' or the 'emotional'. We are all (or very nearly all) *born* with biological sex, but as Simone de Beauvoir famously pointed out, in the case of women, we *become* a gender.[29] Sociologists may once have assumed a straightforward progress from biology to the social, from male to masculinity and from female to femininity, but nobody living in the contemporary West (sociologist or not) now assumes such an unproblematic progression. Feminism, gay politics, psychoanalysis and everyday experience have all made the point that our individual progress from infant male or female to adult *persona* is a complex path. Thus gender, and thinking about gender, inherently disturbs the social world, since we now recognize (even if we do not accept) that masculinity and femininity are not *natural* but *acquired*. Hence the human subject of sociology has to be approached with care: we are no longer the docile creatures with those clear labels of 'woman' and 'man' but human beings whose sexuality and sexual identity we know to be unstable and complex. Furthermore, we are invited – most clearly by Judith Butler – to consider the idea that not only is gender not natural but it is the social foundation of a deeply divided and unequal social world. Butler writes:

> The economic, tied to the reproductive, is necessarily linked to the reproduction of heterosexuality. It is not that non-heterosexual forms of sexuality are simply left out, but that their suppression is essential to the operation of that prior normativity. This is not simply a question of certain people suffering a lack of cultural recognition by others but, rather, a specific mode of sexual production and exchange that works to maintain the stability of gender, the heterosexuality of desire, and the naturalization of the family.[30]

Butler's views about the appropriate nature of politics (both feminist and otherwise) have been the subject of debate and scrutiny.[31] Sufficient to say here that whatever conclusion we might come to about the political implications of her work, one intellectual implication is clear and widely accepted: that gender is not the stable identity which was once assumed.

However, when Marx, Weber, Durkheim and Simmel wrote about women they wrote with confidence about the meaning of the word which had remained largely undisturbed since the time of Plato, whose *Republic* had set out a view of women, and the 'nature' of women, that had informed educated thinking for generations:

> To conclude, then, there is no occupation with the management of social affairs which belongs either to woman or to man, as such. Natural gifts are to be found here and there in both creatures alike; and every occupation is open to both, so far as their natures are concerned, though woman is for all purposes the weaker.[32]

For centuries the West (both female and male) took for granted 'natural' differences between the sexes. When eighteenth-century women claimed, in the phrase used by Londa Scheibinger, that 'the mind has no sex' they were reasserting, rather than stating for the first time, women's claims to participation in intellectual life.[33] Thus the issue about women's relationship to the social world was not that of the assumption that women were intellectually inferior, but that the form which women's interests and inclinations took was different from that of men. When Anne Elliot in Jane Austen's *Persuasion* argued that: 'Men have had every advantage of us telling their own story. Education has been theirs in so much higher a degree; the pen has been in their hands'[34] she was claiming the continued recognition of women's intellectual and moral abilities.

The nineteenth century increasingly saw the articulation of the view that the mind *did* have a sex, and that women's minds – as Hegel claimed in *The Philosophy of Right* – were constructed through 'feminine' qualities of intuition, affection and subjectivity.[35] These qualities, while essential in the family, had, according to Hegel, no place in public ethical life. It was this account of women, and the view of men as creatures of objectivity and rationality, that informed many nineteenth-century discussions of women, not least those of the 'Great Old Men' of sociology. The thesis proposed by Hegel was not, however, about the intellectual inferiority of women, but about the intellectual *inclination* of women: this was not a debate about capacity, but about the direction and the form of intellectual competence. Marx did not radically disturb existing ideas about the 'natural' differences between women and men, although his disturbance of ideas about the social space to be occupied by women and men was radical. (Indeed, as Simone de Beauvoir recognized in the penultimate paragraph of *The Second Sex*, Marx used the analogy of the ideal relation between men and women to make his point about the ideal relationship between all human beings: 'The direct, natural necessary relation of human creatures is the relation of man to women'.)[36] But Weber, Durkheim and Simmel all recognized more about sexual difference than Marx: they recognized the constructed states of masculinity and femininity. This crucial step allowed them all, but most particularly Durkheim and Simmel, to relate gender difference to different objective and subjective experiences of the social world. In *The Division of Labour in Society* Durkheim takes the theoretically crucial step of suggesting that human beings change and develop in different ways according to the nature of the society – and particularly the status of the division of labour – within which they live. In Durkheim's account of the history of the relations between women and men there is a transition from 'completely rudimentary' marriage to a far more complex and important institution: 'The union of two people has ceased to be ephemeral; it is no longer an external contract temporary and partial, but an intimate association, lasting, often even in-dissoluble during the whole lifetime of the two parties'.[37]

The paragraphs which follow this statement contain a remarkable mix of the highly contentious and the unremarkable. Durkheim points out that 'Today, among cultivated people, the woman leads a completely different existence from that of the man', and goes on to suggest that women, like men, are carrying out their own 'nature'.[38] For the nineteenth-century bourgeoisie throughout Europe the differentiation of social experience for women and men was, in many cases, considerable. But it is a matter of historical record that women and men outside this class often worked in similar conditions of hardship and poverty, just as bourgeois women and men worked together in particular situations. Thus the empirical basis for Durkheim's comments about the different social experiences of women and men is only partially correct. More important is his thesis that the 'con-jugal solidarity' of cultivated people, created out of sexual differentiation, underpins moral solidarity.[39] It is this argument that confronts us, in the twenty-first century, as of lasting importance, since we live (in the West) in societies in which material and cultural forces increasingly diminish and marginalize sexual differentiation. The question that, following Durkheim, we would have to ask concerns the social and moral consequences of gender 'de-differentiation'.

This is hardly a question which has been widely discussed by feminists, since for many (although not all) the cause of women's emancipation rests upon the twofold assumption that differences between women and men are constructed (and can therefore be changed) and that gender differentiation (and specialization of function) is a feature not of a 'cultivated' society, as Durkheim argued, but of a backward-looking one. Nevertheless, the issue of the relationship between gender de-differentiation and moral disintegration

remains, if not actually persuasive to feminists, at least theoretically interesting. Equally interesting, and equally theoretically important, is Simmel's
account of the relationship between gender and culture. Many years before
second-wave feminists and others, both male and female, had taken issue
with the identification of white men with objectivity, Simmel wrote in *The
Problem of the Sexes* that: 'The male sex is not merely superior in relation
to the female but acquires the status of the *generally human*, governing the
phenomena of the individual male and the individual female in the same
way'.[40]

It is Simmel's articulation of the taken-for-granted assumption that men
are culture (in the same way as women are nature and 'saturated with
sexuality') that places his work as central to discussions of gender and
social theory. The passage above was written in 1923; several generations
later, critics of racism and sexism in western universalistic theories of knowledge were to echo many of the ideas proposed by Simmel. Thus Henrietta
Moore, for example, takes issue with the implicit (and as she suggests
unthinking) masculine bias in anthropology, just as Luce Irigaray was to
voice the view that women are a sex 'which is not one' and that:

> For woman is traditionally use-value for man, exchange-value
> among men. Merchandise, then. This makes her the guardian of
> matter whose price will be determined by 'subjects': workers,
> tradesmen, consumers, according to the standard of their work
> and their need-desire. Women are marked phallically by their
> fathers, husbands, procurers. This stamp(ing) determines their
> value in sexual commerce. Woman is never anything more than
> the scene of more or less rival exchange between two men, even
> when they are competing for the possession of mother-earth.[41]

Irigaray's essay (first published in 1977) was primarily concerned with
sexual, rather than social, relationships. But what she disturbed were two
narratives about sexuality which up to that point had dominated much
thinking about sexuality. The first was that of Freud: a narrative about
sexuality and sexual development which allowed for the complexity of
sexual and psychic development but also assumed heterosexuality as the
organizing structure of desire. The second and far more general narrative
was that of the naturalization of sexuality. This rhetoric took for granted
the equation of male/female biology with the genders of masculinity and
femininity. As Kate Millett wrote in 1971, 'patriarchy has a . . . tenacious
or powerful hold through its successful habit of passing itself off as nature'.[42]
Feminism both attacked arguments about gender drawn from nature, and
naturalization, and at the same time, through writers such as Adrienne
Rich, argued for natural sexual difference.[43] Nevertheless, by 1990 it was
possible for Kate Soper to write that 'feminism as theory has pulled the rug
from under feminism as politics'.[44] The disappearance of 'womanhood', as

Soper pointed out, was indicative of a general, late twentieth-century movement from solidarity to individualism.

The consensus among feminists at the beginning of the twenty-first century is that nature, and the natural, are at best unreliable guides to behaviour. Sociology, whose business has always been the demonstration of the impact of the created social world on human agency, has traditionally been more sceptical about 'nature' than feminism: there was no political or theoretical ground to be gained by sociologists in giving way to explanations from nature. Indeed, the whole enterprise of sociology was to denaturalize our understanding of the world, and to emphasize the social rather than the natural. In that endeavour lay sociology's original radicalism: a radicalism which was of course revealed as partial by feminists, who could point only too clearly at comments by the Grand Old Men of sociology which took for granted 'natural' differences and inclinations between women and men. Taking back (or more accurately gaining in the first place) the theoretical ownership of gender was the first task for both feminist and gay sociologists. The implications of the socialization of gender for social theory are the subject of the following chapters.

CHAPTER 2

THE MEANING OF WORK

It is conventional to assume that modern social theory is a post-Enlightenment phenomenon, and one in which European traditions fused to produce those dynamic accounts of the social world of Comte, Marx, Weber and Durkheim. In some histories of social theory, particularly those with a more developed sense of history, there is also a discussion of the impact of Charles Darwin on theories of social change, and subsequently of Sigmund Freud on questions related to the relationship of the individual and society. But few women intrude in this canon of social theory; still less is it suggested that social theory in the nineteenth (and much of the twentieth) century had anything to say about relationships between women and men.[1] (Exceptions to the absence of dicussions of gender in the genesis of social theory are to be found in Larry Ray's *Theorizing Classical Sociology* and the work of Anne Witz and Barbara Marshall.)

The dominant issues of the nineteenth and early twentieth centuries were those of social change, social class and social cohesion. Social inequalities are assumed to have preoccupied those venerable nineteenth- and early twentieth-century sages of the social world. But if we return to the nineteenth century, and to its earliest years, we find women writing accounts of the social world, and in particular accounts of the relationship of gender to the construction of knowledge, which are every bit as relevant to the twenty-first century as they were to the period of pre-industrial, post-Enlightenment Europe. Mary Wollstonecraft and Mary Shelley (mother and daughter) are seldom included in conventional accounts of social theory, but what they both had to say about knowledge and gender has become, albeit largely implicitly, part of our western cultural heritage. In this assertion – hopefully heretical to those with rigid and fixed ideas about the nature and meaning of theory – is contained the view that the idea of 'theory' has to be both deconstructed and reconstructed.

The deconstruction must remove some of the firm boundaries imposed between 'theory' and the rest, while the reconstruction must allow that discussions of the social world are many and various and are informed by various traditions and resources. In the later part of the twentieth century, social theory became firmly part of the academy: a discourse which was (and is) the preserve of professional academics within an institutional context. But the earliest great names of sociological theory wrote from locations either distant from, or only partially engaged in, the academy. As such, their work did not have to meet those requirements which have – to later theorists – imposed strangleholds of relevance and the professional audience on their work. So in 'reconstructing' theory to allow a more inclusive discussion of those who have something to say about the social world, I do not wish to suggest that these newly included figures (for example Wollstonecraft and Shelley) influenced in any known or demonstrable way Comte *et al.*, but that at this very first point of a discussion of gender and sociological theory we should allow our definition of 'theory' to be more inclusive and more eclectic than it has been in the past. This is, in short, a suggestion that we should not look back at the past through the lens of the present day rigidities and conventions of the academy (and academic sociology), but look at the past in terms of the figures within it, as a place in which various people attempted to make sense of, to theorize, their social existence. In particular, I should like to propose that nineteenth- and much of twentieth-century social theory written by men was informed by a rigid sense of the 'natural' differences between women and men. This does not make, as some feminist sociologists would argue, canonical theory irrelevant to women, since all members of all human societies are part of the material and symbolic structures of those societies. But we have to recognize that the female person, and the actual and perceived differences resulting from female biology, created a sense of biological difference which was shared by both male and female writers. In general, writers of fiction (male or female) were prepared to suggest more dissent, competition and potential for mutual change than writers of non-fiction, who generally minimized the conflicts of personal life in favour of a discussion of *social* dissent.

At this point it is relevant to raise the question of when is a theory a theory: at what point does writing about the social world become 'theoretical'? Here I would argue that one of the intellectual liberations made possible by second-wave feminism is the idea of the theoretical as narrative. A number of feminist writers (Nancy Armstrong, Sandra Harding, Alice Jardine, Donna Haraway and others) have suggested that within the natural and social sciences, just as much as within fiction, there are 'narratives' about the social world: that the supposedly 'theoretical' and 'objective' is as much a *mélange* of the subjective and the descriptive as any work of fiction. Nancy Armstrong, for example, has suggested the ways in which fiction informed eighteenth- and early nineteenth-century political science: 'Whenever the rhetorical operations of the contract became apparent, as they did to some extent in Hume's essay but even more so in Bentham's *The Theory of Fictions* that power that could be exercised through fictions of personal development also became apparent as such'.[2] Sandra Harding, Donna Haraway, Hilary Rose, Sarah Franklin (and again many others) have argued, in ways similarly informed by ideas about the interdependence and the interrelationship of 'facts' and 'fictions' about the social world, that social theory is informed by ideas about gender.[3] What they have shown, in fact, is that there is no such thing as a genderless social theory.

To say that all theory is gendered has to be immediately qualified and explained. Harding *et al.* are not, emphatically, saying that what we describe as 'science' is 'male' or 'masculinist'. Nor do Harding *et al.* suggest that science, or the 'rational', is for men and against women in any simple or direct sense. The relationship between gender, science and theory is more complex, and for an explanation of exactly how much more complex – and in what ways – it is useful to return to mother and daughter, to Wollstonecraft and Shelley. Mary Wollstonecraft is known throughout the West for *A Vindication of the Rights of Women*, a lengthy assertion that women should not be excluded from the model of citizenship emerging in late eighteenth- and early nineteenth-century Europe.[4] Wollstonecraft demanded the education of women and their inclusion in the public world. But she also demanded – and it is a demand which is frequently forgotten – the inclusion of *men* in the *domestic* world. She argued for the domestication of men just as much as she argued for the education of women.

When Wollstonecraft died (giving birth to Mary) she bequeathed to the world a text which was as much an inspiration for its title as for the details of its pages. Most histories of western feminism date the beginning of modern feminism from 1792, the date of the publication of the *Vindication*. But although the association of the *Vindication* with feminism is very strong, there is in many ways an equally important relationship here – that between the *Vindication* and theories of gender relations, since Wollstonecraft was not merely concerned with changes in the situation of women (and attitudes to them) but also with changes in the behaviour and attitudes of men. As suggested above, she did not simply argue for the inclusion of women in the public world, but also suggested a rearrangement of the social world in which boundaries between the public and private were not demarcated by differences in gender. In her Introduction to the *Vindication* she wrote of the 'barren blooming' of women. By this, she was referring to what she perceived as the process through which strength and usefulness in women were sacrificed (often by women themselves) to beauty. Wollstonecraft continued that: . . . 'the civilised women of the present century, with a few exceptions, are only anxious to inspire love, when they ought to cherish a nobler ambition, and by their abilities and virtues exact respect'.[5] Wollstonecraft clearly did not accept the idea that women were simply victims of male power: contained in the passage above (and throughout the *Vindication*) is a sense of the agency of women (and the negative consequences of that agency) which is often overlooked.

Important as the *Vindication* may have been in feminist history, its immediate impact was limited to the literate and educated in the English population. English (and European) politics were dominated at the time by wealthy white men, and no agenda for the rethinking of the gendered boundaries of politics would be endorsed by any major political party in the late nineteenth century.[6] But Mary Wollstonecraft, like her daughter Mary Shelley, recognized the impact of gender on the ways in which we behave towards each other and (most particularly in the case of Mary Shelley) the way in which we construct information about the social world. In Shelley's *Frankenstein*, a monster ('the Creature' of the novel) is created through science and scientific inquiry. The capacities for the scientific exploration of the universe which Frankenstein demonstrates arise out of mixed motives, but one is more crucial than the others: the desire, on Frankenstein's part, to create life and to demonstrate that Man (in this case literally) can give birth to human beings. But 'the Creature', denied human parenting and human society, becomes a victim to his own needs and desires. Man and monster destroy each other.

In *Frankenstein* there are, as in any great text, complex meanings and complex influences. There are, in this case as in others, diverse interpretations. In this context, however, two interpretations – in the sense of two recognitions of Shelley's arguments – are possible. The first is that Mary Shelley recognized the power of science, knowledge and scientific inquiry. But Shelley's recognition is critical, and in particular she is critical, as Gillian Beer has observed, of early nineteenth-century accounts of science and scientists which put in place a 'glorious narrative' of scientific discovery as the motive for discovery and conquest.[7] As Beer points out:

> Mary Shelley's approach to her discoverer Walton is unmistakably sardonic. She portrays him as a spoilt young egotist who complains continuously to the patient sister he has left behind, and all along risks the lives of the family men who make up his crew. Mary Shelley's reaction to science of this kind has some similarities to that of the modern physicist Brian Easlea, as he examines the psychic investments and public policy behind the twentieth century arms race. 'Modern science is basically a masculine endeavour, and in a world of competing nation states and blocs serves to fuel the fires of human conflict rather than to quench them'.[8]

Mary Shelley did not simply recognize the power of science in terms of its possible (albeit negative) creativity, she also recognized the seductive appeal of knowledge. Thus the second recognition for which we must honour Shelley is that she understood the difficulties in the relationship between science, the pursuit of knowledge and what might be described as 'the rational' and those other issues associated with morality and the authority once given to God. In taking up the cause of science, Frankenstein appeared to be taking on the mantle of the perfect hero of the Enlightenment. Yet in refusing to entertain the moral questions surrounding his actions, he plunged himself, and his family, into those horrors (of destruction and the rule of the mob) which were to be replicated in the twentieth century. Numerous theorists of the social world – members of the Frankfurt School and Zygmunt Baumann in particular – have argued for the close connection between the Holocaust and modernity.[9] Baumann's claim, widely discussed and reiterated, is that the resolute ruthlessness of 'modern' organization and its attitudes created those capacities and expectations which made possible the attempted destruction of European Jewry. It is a powerful thesis, and one echoed in studies such as that of Adorno on the irrational in modernity.[10] Yet the theoretical interpretations of the history of the past 200 years which these men have offered covered the same ground – within a different discourse – as that of Mary Shelley.

Shelley's 'Creature', unloved and untutored by mother or father, is the human (or at least living) personification of the monstrous possibilities of science and rational inquiry. At the beginning of the twenty-first century the creation of Dolly the sheep (on this occasion a female rather than male creation) demonstrates the fulfilment of Shelley's fiction. We now have a 'real' living mammal which has been artificially created, yet at the same time we are still faced with the same moral and social issues which confronted Frankenstein and Mary Shelley. As Sarah Franklin has pointed out, questions remain about whether or not it is morally acceptable to create life artificially, as well as asking those more materially related questions about the use of expensive scientific resources for such exercises.[11] Mary Shelley suggested in Frankenstein that the wish to create life artificially was a specifically male one, born (as it were) out of men's inability to give birth. Debates about science – and in particular about new technologies of reproduction – still cover similar ground, a ground in which the scientific and scientific inquiry are associated with the male, as is the wish to control the results of that inquiry.

This digression into a discussion of the birth of the best known monster in European history is to illustrate a point about the relationship of the imagination to theory. Mary Shelley did not, in our accepted understanding of the term, 'theorize', but she did *imagine*, and the force of that imaginative vision remains with us 150 years after her death. Our present-day pattern of organizing knowledge is one in which we distinguish between fiction and non-fiction, between the imagined and the theoretical, as well as making conventional distinctions between those subjects studied in schools

and universities. Not making those distinctions would probably inconveni-
ence the institutional construction of knowledge but maintaining them –
particularly for those interested in the order and working of human society
– underpins our failure to recognize the strength of the world of the imagination and its relationship to what we assume to be the 'real world'. In
many ways, this renders theoretical accounts of the social and the interper-
sonal world as distant and, in a fundamental sense, alien to human experience. That fundamental sense is the refusal, in aspects of social theory, to
recognize that we may be capable of abstract, theoretical, apparently rational thought, but we do not all act in consistently rational ways all the
time. We are the products, not just of a social world, but of a personal
world as well. If, as Nancy Armstrong has suggested, 'the modern individual is first and foremost a woman' then we can appreciate the motiva-
tional diversity of human action, since women – following Armstrong – are
allowed (and expected) to unite rationality and sensibility.[12]

When we begin to rethink the history of post-Enlightenment social theory
in terms of gender, we can begin to see more clearly the stresses and fault
lines in social theory, since the informing gaze of gender locates the discrep-
ancy between accounts of the public world and those of the private world.
Indeed, if we see the modern individual as female rather than male we can
see that much of canonical social theory, while written in terms of the male
subject, is nevertheless concerned with a condition more generally equated
with women – that of subjectivity. Rereading through this lens allows us to
see Weber's *The Protestant Ethic and the Spirit of Capitalism* or Durkheim's
Suicide as attempts to engage with the understanding of human subjectivity. However, the intellectual history of Europe was not one in which the
institutional organization of knowledge transgressed or confused the conventional order of gender and knowledge. On the contrary, the order of
knowledge, its institutions and its expectations, moved gradually, but systematically, towards greater specialization and more rigid, and final, separa-
tions. At the beginning of the nineteenth century, women such as Mary
Wollstonecraft and Mary Shelley had been able to take part in a relatively
informal intellectual life, and in so doing bequeathed to the world works of
lasting relevance. By the end of the nineteenth century, entry to intellectual
life was largely channelled through the universities so that the chances of
the untutored becoming part of the creative process of intellectual life had
become, in many areas of inquiry, minimal. Foucault is well known for
advancing an account of the relentless progress towards the bureaucratic
organization of knowledge in the nineteenth century; his account emphasizes the institutional, whereas here an emphasis is important on the gradual,
yet marked, gendering of knowledge and the increasing boundary maintenance between the world of fiction and non-fiction.[13] Both these shifts had
implications for gender and social theory which remain with us to this day
and suggest that more pessimistic views of the relationship between women

and the Enlightenment, most significantly that of Catherine Belsey, might be more accurate than that of Armstrong. Belsey wrote: 'The Enlightenment commitment to truth and reason, we can now recognise, has meant historically a single truth and a single rationality, which have conspired in practice to legitimate the subordination of women'.[14]

If the *ideas* of the Enlightenment were to become restrictive in their impact on the intellectual and imaginative life of women (or more particularly expectations about it), then there is equally a case for arguing that the form of social relations which evolved in the West in the nineteenth century – that of a capitalist market economy – was equally problematic for women. However, the great theorist of industrial capitalism, Karl Marx, was one of the first to perceive that capitalism, while seldom explicitly positive for women, nevertheless offered hitherto unknown possibilities for them. A great deal of ink has now been spilt on the subject of whether or not Marx and Marxism are both gender-blind and gender-irrelevant, but those debates (notably about the question of whether or not the unpaid work of women contributes to productive or unproductive labour) should not obscure the concern of both Marx and Engels with the question of gender relations.[15] That concern is most explicitly discussed in Engels' *The Origin of the Family, Private Property and the State*. Although the relevance of this text to the twentieth and twenty-first centuries has been questioned, it remains central to discussions about the social role of women, not least because Engels' analysis, as Michele Barrett has pointed out, 'was "codified" into a blueprint for the emancipation of women'.[16] That 'blueprint' was first espoused by state socialist societies, but more recently has been endorsed by western, capitalist societies eager to end what is constructed as the 'dependence' of non-wage earning women on the state.

It is deeply ironic that contemporary capitalism has become as enthusiastic about the entry of women into production as the most avowedly Marxist state socialist society, and as fervent in its equation of women's entry into production with 'emancipation' and 'liberation'. In this enthusiasm, which places the state of Massachussetts almost on a par with Stalin's Russia in terms of its policies about women and paid work, the greater part of Marx's work – indeed, the discussion of the very context in which we live and work – is lost. (It also provides a telling example of the way in which women as a group can be used to signify social progress and modernization without any reference to the wider historical context.) In general, however, academic feminism has in the past tended to follow the old Soviet Union in terms of the way in which Marx's work is viewed. That is, there is considerable material about the issue of whether or not housework, care for others and unpaid household work in general contributes 'productive' or 'unproductive' work in terms of Marx's construction of these terms. To these debates, significant contributions have come from Veronica Beechey and Hilary Wainwright.[17] There have also been contributions (for example

from Sonia Kruks) on the issue of women's general position in state socialist societies.[18] Recently, Barbara Einhorn is among those who have provided accounts of the impact of the post-1989 transformations in eastern
Europe on women.[19] Among the most engaging and informative of the
rereadings of Marx by feminists in the 1970s was that by Irene Bruegel,
who took the term 'reserve army of labour' from Marx and made it into a
description specifically about the relationship of women to the capitalist
mode of production.[20]

The extensive work of academics on Marx now includes, therefore, feminist rereadings of Marx and Engels. However, in the main, those readings
emphasize the economic and the material in Marx's work: his account of
paid work, production and the workings of capital. Women have now been
located in Marx and Engels largely in the context of debates about paid
and unpaid work. But in this reading of Marx I would emphasize two
points: the first is that academic feminism of the 1970s and 1980s read
Marx through a lens of gender, but a lens defined in terms of a stress on the
discussion of the organization of production in Marx's work. Just as Marxist scholarship was moving towards a more nuanced interpretation of Marx
– and postmodernism was emphasizing what could be salvaged in Marx's
work for accounts of urban life in late modernity – feminism largely saw
Marx as a theorist of production, rather than a more general theorist of
social relations.[21] This led to a second consequence of a particular reading
of Marx – the general abandonment of Marxist readings and analyses of
late capitalism in favour of readings derived from cultural politics (where
gender is an essential element) rather than class politics (where gender
sits more uneasily). Debates of the late 1970s between Christine Delphy,
Mary McIntosh, Diana Leonard and Michele Barrett demonstrated the difference between feminists about the importance of social class in feminist
analysis and the strength of feeling, on both sides of the debate, about the
issue.[22]

It is not, however, the case that Marx writes solely or exclusively about
social class, and still less that he writes about social class in the sense
understood by the majority of social scientists. The terms 'working class'
and 'middle class' are not part of a Marxist vocabulary, and arguably far
more important are those descriptions of social class more generally used
by Marx – terms such as 'bourgeois', 'proletariat' and 'petit-bourgeois'.
What these terms suggest is the complexity of relations between classes, an
idea largely lost in the more static 'working class' and 'middle class' and yet
of potent interest to anyone concerned with questions of gender and class.
It is thus on the questions of the links between classes and on the links
between classes and the reproduction of capitalist social relations in general
that we can find an intersection between Marx and ideas about gender.
Marx, it has to be said, did not disturb nineteenth-century ideas about
sexual difference and took for granted 'natural' relationships between women

and men, and women and children. He did not participate in that disturbance of sexual identity which was to become part of social theory and social experience in the twentieth century. 'Gay' modernity was not part of Marx's agenda for the future development of capitalist society, let alone a possible transforming part of it.

Between 1843 and 1883 Marx bequeathed to the world an account of the emergence and the dynamic of the social world in which mid-Victorians lived. He was hardly alone in recognizing both the political turmoil of those years (as partially democratic assemblies battled for their right to rule against entrenched aristocratic interests) and the social and material transformation that was taking place. Of the period 1848–75, E.J. Hobsbawm has written:

> The history of our period is therefore lopsided. It is primarily that of the massive advance of the world economy of industrial capitalism, of the social order which it represented, of the ideas and beliefs which seemed to legitimise and ratify it: in reason, science, progress and liberalism. It is the era of the triumphant bourgeois, though the European bourgeoisie still hesitated to commit itself to public political rule.[23]

Marx, like many other people of his era, wanted to understand this new world, and in attempting to do so he turned, like many before him, to an account of the earliest years of human society. Our emergence from barbarism and the Stone Age was, according to Marx, achieved through the domestication of animals and the construction of social ideas about the inheritance of property. With this social order came patriarchy: the organization of the world into a place which gave precedence to the authority of men. Men inherited property, men became rulers and women became, if not immediately the 'angels of the house' (as Virginia Woolf described bourgeois women of nineteenth-century England), at least the inhabitants of a different social place – the home. The 'polis', the public world, was the realm of men, as was the understanding (certainly in the work of Aristotle and Plato) which went with it.

As with other aspects of Marx's work, there are now volumes on his anthropology, his account of history and his theory of social change. In general, the consensus about Marx's grasp of anthropology is that it is limited, but largely correct, in its recognition of the impact on gender relations of the end of hunter gatherer societies and the emergence of settled societies. Nothing in Marx's investigations of subsequent European history suggests that he returned to re-examining or reconsidering an account of the past which essentially took for granted the distinction between the public world of men and the private world of women. However, once faced with the reality of gender relations in his own era, Marx assumed both a 'natural' relationship between women and children, and the expectation that a socialist revolution would solve the 'woman question'. In one of his more celebrated passages Marx argued for monogamy as that form of heterosexual relations which most benefits women. Equally, and in the same context, he remarked that a society could be judged in terms of its degree of social progress by the extent to which it had emancipated women. This established a firm link for all later readers and sympathizers with Marx's work between female emancipation and social evolution. But what is crucially significant here are two points: first, that for Marx, and even more so for Engels, the emancipation of women was defined by the extent to which women entered social production (and hence, for Marx, social relations and the social world). Second, that Marx did not disturb or challenge given distinctions between male and female, man and woman, husbands and wives. Not for Marx the disturbance of sexual (as opposed to social) identity which became a part of social theory in the twentieth century.

The link which Marx and Engels established between women's emancipation and their entry into social production has been, as suggested above, of interest to academics. In a rather more socially significant way, the thesis was accepted by state socialist societies. In the Soviet Union between 1917–89 the constitution assumed that both women and men would enter 'productive' labour, and to underpin this assumption the state (both in the old Soviet Union and its satellite states) put into place extensive systems of nursery schools and other forms of provision for the care of children. It was a model replicated in Communist China. This form of social organization certainly allowed women with children access to what in the West is described as the 'labour market', but it did not radically alter the distribution of social power in any state socialist society. Western feminists in the 1970s and early 1980s looked to the East and found precisely the kind of extensive child care facilities which women in the West were demanding, but also found a 'double shift' worked by women which was accompanied by the replication of wholly familiar patterns of the concentration of power and privilege in male hands.[24]

Debates about gender relations in state socialist societies did not occur, however, for some time after Marx's death. The essential heritage of Marx for sociological theory lay not in his account of gender relations but in his account of class relations and the social dynamic which creates and reproduces them. Few (if any) male writers have studied Marx in terms of his contribution to discussions about gender, but, as suggested above, a rather more considerable literature exists by feminists about Marx on women. There is no discussion in Marx about 'gender' *per se*, since this is a term not widely used until the late twentieth century, and the occasions in his work when he addresses ideas about sexual difference are few and far between. (For example, in *The Economic and Philosophic Manuscripts of 1844* he recognizes the prostitution of the wives and daughters of impoverished male factory workers, but this idea is located securely within the

context of heterosexuality, male sexual 'needs' and patriarchal constructions of morality.)[25] But while Marx accepts Engels' dictum that in the
family the wife is the proletariat and the husband the bourgeois, this remark is heavily qualified by both men (although less so by subsequent
feminists who seized on it as an indication of Marx's recognition of the
subordination of women) by the placing of individual families securely and
firmly within a class structure. Thus while a bourgeois woman might well
be a 'proletarian' in terms of the internal organization of her family (and certainly at the time Marx was writing would have had as few legal and civil
rights as a woman from a proletarian family) she had access to, and enjoyed,
the privileges of her class.

This issue gave rise, as we have seen, to fierce debates within feminism
about the 'class' of women and the meaning of productive and unproductive labour. The literature of the debate returned frequently to a discussion
of Marx, whose words were held up for Talmudic re-examination. Whatever the academic conclusion of the debate (and probably it is best summed
up as a conclusion in which it was agreed, if tacitly, that the debate depended upon entirely incompatible readings of Marx) it did have massively
important practical consequences in that first and foremost, unpaid domestic and caring work was more fully and publically recognized; and second
that this work began to be rewarded, in many western societies, by financial
benefits. Hilary Land, Hilary Graham and Clare Ungerson were just three
of the feminist academics who demonstrated the centrality of unpaid work
to the continuation of the social world and social relations within the family.[26] The link, in this case, between what began as an academic debate and
real material results is a very clear one.

Thus in the case of the work of Marx, what we can see in terms of a
particular concern with gender, and gender relations, is an engagement
with Marx's theoretical vocabulary and theory of society in order to illuminate particular areas of feminist concern. Male theorists have 'used' Marx
to develop theories of social power, social change, globalization and political economy (here the list of names would run for pages), while female
theorists have turned to Marx in order to find theoretical structures to
illuminate the social position of women. What is important here is the idea
of 'reading' Marx which was part of the feminist rediscovery of his work in
the 1970s and 1980s. The idea of 'reading' emerged from theoretical traditions and developments in literary criticism, traditions themselves inspired
by structuralism and deconstruction. 'Reading' Marx allowed feminists and
others to suggest interpretations that gave a greater degree of freedom from
the literal. Above all else, 'reading' allowed the idea that no text is stable,
that words do not always carry fixed and single unambiguous meanings.
For example, two significant instances of 'reading' in the 1970s were Louis
Althusser's *Reading Capital* and Juliet Mitchell's *Psychoanalysis and Feminism*. Published in 1974, *Psychoanalysis and Feminism* was a rereading of

Freud, inspired and informed by the idea that Freud had a great deal to say about women, men and relations between the sexes which had not been allowed by previous interpretations.[27]

In the 1970s, therefore, there was a considerable 'return' to Marx, made possible by the availability of his work in English and by the inspiration of postmodernist interpretations of the world which allowed for, and encouraged, more heterogeneous and diverse accounts of the social and the symbolic. What David Harvey and others described as the 'death of grand theory' also made possible its rediscovery and its re-evaluation.[28] Because it was no longer assumed that a reading of Marx would only be allied with a single politics and a single theoretical direction, it was possible to draw on Marx (and Freud) for inspiration. Marx, like Freud, was no longer (by the end of the 1980s) taken to task for ignoring women (although the case in terms of gender and masculinity remained considerable), for two reasons: first, it had been established that Marx, on occasions, *did* address directly questions about women and sexual inequality; and second, the nature of the theoretical had changed. No longer was sociological theory (or feminist theory) to be confined to the realms of the public space or the literal comment. On the contrary, the sociological theory which emerged from the 1980s was one which allowed the private world as much as the public, and the unsaid and the symbolic as much as the said and the material.

In this context, discussions of gender and sexual inequality have developed aspects of Marx's work in ways which would have been impossible without shifts in the meaning of the theoretical. Most significantly, the idea of 'social capital' has become part of our understanding of the way in which gender and class are related. The work of Pierre Bourdieu, which in itself draws on the work of Marx, has been developed by Beverley Skeggs and Terry Lovell to show how the relationship between class and gender might be interpreted and fused.[29] No longer, therefore, is there an assumption that we have to choose either class or gender in order to define social experience and social identity. What is also part of the theoretical world of Bourdieu, Skeggs and Lovell is the shift in the understanding of the social world itself: from a world in which production was paramount to a world in which consumption is assumed to be of central importance. However, in this assumption there lies an intellectual and political difference which it is impossible to overlook, and which I would argue is crucial to any social understanding of the world of the twenty-first century. The issue is that of the question of whether or not (as Fukuyama has put it) history has ended, and whether, in particular, class and class antagonism (in the structural rather than the strictly personal sense) have disappeared.[30] To many sociologists, class in Marx's sense is dead, as is any social theory which proposes that the structural class inequalities suggested by Marx remain.

Bourdieu, Lovell, Skeggs and others do not take this view. They recognize that the West of the twenty-first century is a different place from the

England of the nineteenth century in which Marx lived and worked. The democratization of consumption, underpinned by long periods of full employment and state intervention in welfare and education, has radically diminished the evident social differences and experiences of the populations of the nineteenth century. The manufacturing industries (largely employers of men) have, in many western societies, disappeared and been replaced by new 'industries' of the personal service sector (where labour can be either male or female). Susan Faludi in the USA and Beatrix Campbell in Britain have documented the collapse of traditional patterns of male employment.[31] The 'crisis of masculinity', as it has been described, is seen as having many facets. Evidence about the impact on men of unemployment is one example, but other instances of the contemporary malaise of men are the growing differences in life expectancy between women and men, the high rate of suicide among men (particularly young men) and the differences in success at examinations in secondary school between girls and boys in England and Wales.[32] Popular culture has not been slow to articulate these instances of the contemporary plight of men: the British films *The Full Monty* and *Brassed Off* were both widely successful and both dealt with the impact on men of what sociologists and economists refer to as the 'restructuring' of industry.

When Marx and Engels wrote their accounts of poverty and class inequality they saw the only form of human emancipation – be it for men or women – as lying in the radical restructuring of industry, the creation of socialism and the entry of women into 'social production'. While both Marx and Engels had an educated knowledge of literature and history, their work – while often rich in the discussion of the particular social attitudes and social understanding of given social groups – pays little specific attention to the differences in understanding and experience between women and men. In the twenty-first century this absence of the recognition of gender difference appears as an important oversight: sociologists today are expected to acknowledge the importance of gender differences and to list it as a major form of social differentiation. But in the nineteenth century, discussion of a *social* world which explicitly included women was in itself radical. For Marx and Engels to argue that the integration of women into the social world was an essential part of human and social progress was revolutionary in societies and cultures which assumed that women's place was in the household. Even though there were considerable numbers of women in paid employment in the nineteenth century (as Sally Alexander and other feminist historians have pointed out), social norms assumed that this was both an aberrant and undesirable situation.[33] To Marx and Engels, therefore, we must allow the credit for challenging taken-for-granted assumptions about the social role of women and, by implication (which is more apparent in the twenty-first than the nineteenth century) the nature of relations between the sexes.

The contribution of Marx and Engels to sociology has been discussed extensively elsewhere, and it is not the purpose of this book to review that literature, except to say that what Marx and Engels gave to sociology (and the social sciences, and our understanding of the social world in general) was a theory of social change and the relationship of individuals to that change and the social structure.[34] What it is assumed that they did not do was to integrate into their accounts of the social world a recognition of moral and emotional relationships between individuals. Thus it is all too easy for human beings, read through the eyes of what used to be described as 'vulgar' Marxism, to be reduced to mere ciphers of class position. Bourgeois acts as bourgeois, proletarian acts as proletarian in these accounts. In the years after the death of Marx and Engels many sympathetic to their theory of society attempted to rescue them from their misuse by materialists, but these attempts were often impeded by the absence in the work of both men of a nuanced recognition of the complexity of lived social experience and the possibilities of human agency for positive and negative action. These rescue attempts were particularly apparent in the area of the study of culture: Marxist critics such as George Lukacs took considerable personal and intellectual risks in arguing that Marxism was not necessarily always and inevitably associated with socialist realism or doctrinaire art and literature.[35] Yet readings of Marx can provide wonderfully vivid accounts of the ways in which individuals internalize social values. For example, in the article 'The Power of Money in Bourgeois Society' in *The Economic and Philosophic Manuscripts of 1844* Marx (perhaps thinking of his own physical appearance) speaks of the transforming power of money on the person: 'I am ugly, but I can buy for myself the most beautiful women. Therefore I am not ugly, for the effects of ugliness – its deterrent money – is nullified by money'.[36]

The accounts of the social world bequeathed by Marx and Engels were written at the same time as a number of great English novels by women writers. This point is made not just out of historical interest but because those women writers who were contemporaries of Marx and Engels (Charlotte Brontë, Anne Brontë, Emily Brontë, Elizabeth Gaskell and George Eliot) contributed to another tradition of the understanding of the social world: that of the novel and narrative fiction. The novels they wrote, about the same society as Marx and Engels, give us an understanding of the individual experience of living (as a man or a woman) in Victorian England, even though the novel has often been assumed to be secondary to social documentation in terms of its possibilities for social understanding. Hence in the years after Marx and Engels, as the West established institutional knowledge in the form of structures of education and examination, 'fiction' was consistently placed in a different part of the academy (and the intellectual world in general) from that of the social sciences in general and sociology in particular. But the 'turn to culture' in sociology allows us to consider again these distinctions and to ask if some of the limitations of sociology as a discipline do not come from this premature separation of different forms of knowledge and experience. By way of example, it is instructive to consider two works about the impact of industrialization which were published at about the same time: Elizabeth Gaskell's *North and South* and Friedrich Engels' *The Condition of the Working Class.*

It is apparent that both Gaskell and Engels share an intense concern about the human consequences of the Industrial Revolution. Both document and explore the poverty and misery which is inflicted on individuals through the growth of the factory system and squalid industrial towns. But what Gaskell sees in *North and South* is individual agency (and in particular the agency of women), social relationships, community associations and the possibility of moral choices by individuals which challenge the existence of poverty and deprivation. In the final reconciliation at the end of *North and South* Gaskell allows her two central characters, hero and heroine, to unite in a commitment to the betterment of others. If this sounds an impossibly romantic conclusion – Mills and Boon grafted onto social documentation – it is worth noting that as well as the Industrial Revolution, the nineteenth century in Britain also saw the growth of liberal and civic ideals which were, in part, inspired by the possibilities suggested by literature and the imagination. Gaskell's vision, like that of George Eliot, Charles Dickens, Anne Brontë and Charlotte Brontë, never refused the existence of collective and shared hardship. But it also gave to individual men and women a sense of identity as social agents capable of suggesting radical social change. That possibility was not lost on the more conservative contemporaries of Elizabeth Gaskell and Charlotte Brontë. *Jane Eyre*, Charlotte Brontë's furious challenge to male authority, was regarded by many as a dangerously subversive and radical novel, while Gaskell's *Ruth*, which challenged conventional sexual morality, met a storm of abuse on publication.

The novels of Victorian Britain informed, just as much as Marx and Engels, the social understanding of the time. They also gave to citizens an appreciation of the dynamics of gender relations which was absent from Marx and Engels, and which remained largely absent from sociology until the feminist revolution of the 1970s. Yet what the novels also gave to their readers, both male and female, was a sense of the way in which class and gender interact to create specific individuals, and the part that both these social characteristics can play in determining the outcome of social events. For example, the character of Jane Eyre in Charlotte Brontë's novel of the same name is, for much of the novel, a penniless female orphan. In Marxist terms, she is a member of the proletariat, and doubly disadvantaged by her gender. Nevertheless, by virtue of character, education, individual choice and agency she becomes, by the conclusion of the novel, the definitive moral voice of the novel. In the same way that Fanny Price, in Jane Austen's novel *Mansfield Park*, overturned the patriarchal authority of her uncle, Sir

Thomas Bertram, Jane Eyre effectively reorganizes the internal social and moral hierarchy of Brontë's novel.

It is possible for critics to argue that Brontë and Austen are deluded romantics about the social world, producing fantasies of female empowerment and romance which bear no relation to the 'real' world or its structures. The argument has been made elsewhere that the line between *Jane Eyre* and the novels of Barbara Cartland is a very thin one, and only exists at all due to what is, in effect, the snobbery of literary critics.[37] Whether or not this is the case, what needs to be emphasized here is that social theory in the nineteenth century, in the sense of theoretical ideas about the social world produced by that society, owed as much to values about the social world, and the part that those values should play in that world, as it did to the works of Marx and Engels. The argument here is that literature (and the arts generally) contributed (in a way which is too often overlooked) to the construction of the moral understanding and commitment which informed Marx, Engels and other social theorists. The chain of influence may have been long and at times indirect, but it was nevertheless there. Those critics who regarded, in 1847, *Jane Eyre* as a dangerously radical novel were right to recognize that while no novel in itself could cause social revolution, the articulation of resistance and challenge to the given social order could heighten the prospect of social change. Thus in the nineteenth century we find fiction providing what has come to be known as 'a voice' for the dissatisfactions experienced and lived by women. Gendered identity, commonly recognized by sociologists in the late twentieth century, was articulated powerfully in the nineteenth century and contributed to changing those naturalistic assumptions about gender which underpin Marx and Engels.

While men are men and women are women in Marx and Engels, it is, as already suggested, also the case that both writers allow a degree of social construction in gender roles. Of lasting interest in the work of Marx and Engels is the discussion of the construction of social identity. As suggested above, Marx and Engels did not espouse ideas about gender identity which might suggest an explicit challenge to essentialist ideas about gender, but they did see that individuals, male or female, are made by their social circumstances. Thus their work takes a great step forward in accounts of human beings and their actions: it allows both rational action by individuals of both sexes and it recognizes that we are – to individual and diverse extents – formed by our social world and the social experiences we encounter. That in itself was, for its time, a radical vision of the possibilities of individual human emancipation. Neither man wished women to be subject to the endless quasi-slavery of Victorian patriarchy; nor did they wish men to be regarded as the only possible inhabitants of the social space. If at times their blueprint for the future of gender relations in post-capitalist society reads like a blueprint for serial monogamy and the assumption by the state of the responsibilities of fatherhood, what is allowed here is the possibility that gender relations can be transformed, and are not necessarily a product of unchangeable 'natural' relations.

To Marx and Engels, then, as well as to those writers of fiction such as Tolstoy, Eliot and Flaubert, we owe our present understanding of the essential instability of the relationship between the natural and the social. Marx and Engels contributed to the idea that the social and institutional worlds could be changed. They also raised the question of the extent to which we, as human beings, have 'essential' natures, rather than habits and identities that are formed by the social world. In the years after the death of Marx, Sigmund Freud was to advance a transhistorical and transcultural theory of the development of human emotional life which included a theory of the emergence of civilization, and society, as powerful as that of Marx and Engels. But the point of mentioning Freud here is that he, as much as Marx and Engels, assumed certain givens in human individuals which have only recently been challenged. Marx, Engels and Freud all allowed that differences would emerge between human beings in terms of their different experiences of the social world. For Marx and Engels, the emphasis was clearly on social difference; for Freud the emphasis was on the emotional. Yet all three assumed essential differences between men and women, differences which were, in most senses, unaffected by differences in social or individual experience and could thus be said to be 'natural'. At the end of the twentieth century, Judith Butler (and others) were to suggest that no identity (whether social or sexual) is fixed: in this thesis human beings are wholly, rather than partly, permeable by social and individual experience.[38]

This issue of the relationship between the social and the natural has become a crucial one throughout the social sciences (and indeed culture generally) at the beginning of the twenty-first century. Sociological theory, which for many years assumed that categories of 'male' and 'female' could be taken for granted has now to recognize both a theoretical literature (Butler *et al.*) which argues for the social construction of gender in the most radical sense, and documents the reorganization of many aspects of the social relations of production, and the nature of production itself, which had hitherto been taken for granted.[39] For over 100 years – certainly from about 1870 through to the 1960s – manufacturing industry was the dominant form of production in western societies. But, as suggested above, from the 1960s onwards all western societies experienced a decline in manufacturing industries (in the sense of both their contribution to gross national product and the numbers of people employed within them) and a shift to new forms of employment: the consumer and service sector, and those industries and forms of employment related to the 'new' technology of computing and the global communications industry. Marx had recognized that forms of technology would transform aspects of social relations and this was precisely what occurred in the late twentieth century. Men, who had for several generations 'possessed' skills in mining and engineering, found these skills suddenly devoid of both social and economic capital. The social respect and the income which had once given to many men a standing, both within the private and the public world, disappeared.

Faced with this transformation of the social world, sociology did not, on the whole, turn rapidly to an examination of the 'new' world of work. There is a long tradition, both within the sociology of the USA and Britain of the study of paid work, whether that of the middle class or the working class. The majority of these studies are of men, for the obvious reason that the work was completed before the large-scale shift of women into paid work. Among the most distinguished contributions are Paul Willis' *Learning to Labour*, Huw Beynon's *Working for Ford* and Henriques and Slaughter's *Coal is our Life*. In general, the USA provided studies of socialization into middle-class professions, while Britain provided studies of working-class life.[40] These works, completed and published in the period between 1950 and 1975, provided documentary material about the working lives of men: the appearances of women in these studies was fragmentary. In a previous generation the impact of unemployment on men, and their families, had been documented with unsparing clarity in *Marienthal* by Marie Jahoda and Paul Lazarsfeld.[41]

These studies were all part of a world in which male employment was taken as the cornerstone of both social and personal security. It is significant that the only major classic study in which a woman was centrally involved – *Marienthal* – gave an emphasis to the impact of unemployment which included a discussion of its effect on relations within the family. The breakdown of the family, which was identified as one possible consequence of male unemployment in the 1970s, was discussed some 30 years prior to that decade. What *Marienthal* (and the studies above) all demonstrated was that paid work (be it blue collar or professional) was a major source of social identity for men. The loss of dignity associated with unemployment was stressed by writers within the sociological tradition, even though the most vivid individual cases of the loss of self-respect in unemployment had already been provided within literature. From Dickens to E.M. Forster to George Orwell, English literature presented the detailed and specific evidence of the damage to the person of unemployment and poverty. At the same time as authors could show the destructive possibilities of the loss of paid work, it also has to be said that authors (and very often the same ones) also acknowledged the way in which paid work could 'make' a person. Paid work could enhance morally positive characters just as much as it emboldened the pomposity and the pride of those with more dubious moral qualities. In particular, what fiction on both sides of the Atlantic caught with unparalleled recognition was the creation of the world of the white-collar male worker. George Orwell's George Bowling in *Coming Up For Air* and Sinclair Lewis' Babbitt, in the novel of the same name, are the male embodiments of the petit-bourgeois life and spirit: their work is essentially that of service and subordination and their rewards are limited, yet to these characters (and their real-life counterparts) the twentieth-century capitalist world is one which offers lure and undreamt-of rewards.[42]

This world – of both secure employment and a secure social hierarchy in which any white-collar work was better rewarded (and regarded) than that of the working class – began to disappear at the same time as the world of the male manual worker also underwent seismic shifts. Sociologists speak with confidence and assurance of the shift 'from production to consumption' and 'the move to a service economy', but in terms of the impact of these changes on individual lives, and relationships within families and communities, we know relatively little. We know that in Britain and the USA, forms of working-class, male, manual employment became increasingly marginalized throughout the 1960s and 1970s. At the same time, women in sociology began to study women in paid work (Rosemary Pringle and Miriam Glucksmann are two distinguished examples) and the world of all male work became one which was often claimed to possess a 'macho' culture or a high degree of social exclusivity.[43] As more women came to regard paid work as an inevitable and long-term ingredient of social life (rather than simply as an experience confined to life before marriage), so they found numerous forms of employment highly discriminatory in both their formal and informal practices. Thus the shift of much sociological study in the 1970s and 80s was towards the identification of the replication within the labour market of sexual hierarchies. This involved the demonstration both that there were jobs for women which were less well paid and rewarded than those for men, and that within occupational communities the assumption of the greater importance of male interests and competences marginalized or minimized the contribution of women. Theories about the 'dual labour market' and the 'reserve army of labour' became an important part of sociological reading on the world of work.

In this shift, important and significant as it was, two aspects of the world of paid work tended to be overlooked. The first was that the shift to new forms of paid work did not alter in any way the distribution of wealth in either British or North American society. The 'rich' (the figures who had appeared in the work of C.W. Mills, Kolko *et al.*) or the 'upper class' (who had appeared, on the British side of the Atlantic, in the work of Miliband, Wakeford and Urry) now largely disappeared as a visible social class, whether in the real world or the world of sociological textbooks.[44] Nevertheless, although the 'turn to culture' might have given the impression that the social world of the late twentieth century was one without distinctions of class (but only identity related to gender, age, race or patterns of consumption), less culturally informed evidence demonstrated that the rich were still alive and well. But the turn to culture, and the related feminist intervention in sociology, had largely marginalized this aspect of social relations in favour of an emphasis on other forms of social division and exclusion. The second often forgotten aspect of the world of paid work was that its previous form (that form which assumed all paid work to be male) had included significant amounts of paid work by women, and a much greater intervention in the social world by women, than was sometimes supposed by both male and female sociologists. Any student of cultural studies will know that the book which articulated more firmly than any other the world of the twentieth-century English working class – Richard Hoggart's *The Uses of Literacy* – was also a book which placed women centrally within the social world.[45] 'Richard Hoggart's Granny' became one of the central mythological figures to generations of students of British society and cultural studies, but her importance is arguably as great as the driven worker of Weber's *The Protestant Ethic and the Spirit of Capitalism*. Both figures were formed by a specific set of beliefs and social practices: both stood for the demonstration of the creation of the socialized human being through place and circumstances.

The recognition of the role played by women in the social world (a recognition which has now been officially sanctioned by the inclusion of unpaid domestic labour in estimates of gross national product) suggests that sociology has become more inclusive in its parameters and less concerned with a construction of 'society' as synonymous with the public world of men. In one sense this is demonstrably the case, in that the paid (and unpaid) work of women has been recorded and recognized. But at the same time it is important to ask if this greater inclusiveness has not included a narrowing of the discussion about paid work – namely a loss of that sense of paid work as part of specifically capitalist forms of social relations. The shift to studies of the 'culture' of work has emphasized the sexual relationships and understandings in paid work, but this has arguably been accompanied by a loss of the understanding of the impact of the capitalist 'ethic' on individuals, be they male or female. For example, if our concern in a study of work and the workplace is that of gender relations, then what becomes less significant is a concern with the ways in which the *values* implicit in the social process of paid work are those of capitalism rather than patriarchy. What it has often been difficult for feminist sociologists to recognize is that women, just as much as men, can become the creatures of both the Protestant and the capitalist ethic.

Among those sociologists writing about paid work in the twenty-first century is Arlie Hochschild, whose studies of paid work in the USA have added an important dimension to our understanding of the meaning of work in the present century. In both *The Second Shift* and *The Time Bind*, Hochschild has argued that for many people – both women and men – the world of paid work has become preferable to the world of the household.[46] At work, Hochschild argues, people find respect and recognition. Moreover, in contrast to the often erratic and emotionally demanding relationships within the household (particularly if that household includes young children), the world of work offers secure and negotiable boundaries about the expectations of work. In contrast to the limitless time which can be spent in the household in caring for others (with scant expectation of reciprocity) the world of work offers rewards, recognition and structured reciprocity. The world of work has timetables, routinized tasks and often immediate and tangible rewards. The world of the household and the family is much less likely to offer these assurances: the rewards of long-term personal relationships are often intangible and unpredictable. It is arguable, therefore, that in the twenty-first century, the world of paid work has become the focus for both economic and emotional reward. For many people there were always rewards in work, but the shift in the twenty-first century is perhaps towards a prioritization of the workplace over the home, a reorganization of priorities which is increasingly as true for women as for men. The examination of that shift – and possible explanations for it – are the subject of the next chapter.

CHAPTER 3

THE WORLD OF INTIMACY

One of the most influential texts in sociology in the last decade of the twentieth century was *The Transformation of Intimacy* by Anthony Giddens. In this work Giddens argued for what he described as the 'democratization' of gender relations in the West. In his view, gender relations have become more 'democratic' in the past 50 years. At the same time Giddens made no secret of his view that gender relations *should* have become more democratic: he combined the analytical and the normative in his argument.[1] What he also included was reference to a considerable amount of feminist research: the first half of the book drew on those traditions which had emerged in the universities of the West from the 1970s onwards and were concerned with the examination of the private world of the household and the power relations within it. Thus *The Transformation of Intimacy* is important in the way that it brought together feminist research and more mainstream, conventional sociological arguments about the relationship between the personal, the individual and the social.

The Transformation of Intimacy was published in 1992 and has received considerable attention since that time. The argument about the democratization of relations between women and men has been more widely discussed than the second theme of the book – that the democratization of personal relationships (and although Giddens is mainly concerned with relations between women and men, he also refers to relationships between parents and children) underpins and informs the greater democratization of society as a whole. This second argument merits at least as much attention as the first, since *if* this is the case, then what we can demonstrate is a clear link between a form of cultural change (the loss of the legitimacy of patriarchal domestic authority) and social change. On the other hand, there is another way of interpreting the evidence about the democratization of intimacy, and it is to argue that what we can observe is not the democratization of personal relationships but the *erosion* of distinctions between the private and the personal and, above all else, the centrality of the expectations and aspirations of the market economy in the lives of both men and women. For Giddens' argument about democratization to be convincing, it is essential that both women and men (and Giddens' concern is more or less entirely concerned with heterosexual relationships) are economically active and fully participant members of the public, civic, world. The democratization thesis is thus dependent upon the full participation of women in the workplace and the absence of traditional distinctions between the world of men and the world of women. In this context it is apposite to cite material which demonstrates the increase in the rate of labour force participation by women, together with evidence about those social, entirely 'public', contexts and situations (such as examination success at school) in which women now more fully and successfully participate. At the same time it is important to note that Giddens assumes a distinction between the 'public' and the 'private' which has been the subject of debate and criticism by a long tradition of social theorists, from Marx's comments about the 'bourgeois public sphere' to Nancy Fraser's critique of the concept of the 'public' and Lynn Jamieson's critique of the 'pure relationship'.[2]

But arguments against the democratization thesis can also point to the continuation of traditional patterns of participation by women and men in both household tasks and the more complex – and more socially significant – task of child care. All available evidence suggests that it is still women who perform the greater part of household work and it is still women, rather than men, whose employment is interrupted, if not radically altered, by the birth of children.[3] Equally, whatever the gains by women in some areas of middle management, it is still the case, as Mike Savage has argued, that:

> Although women have moved into those areas of professional and managerial employment in some numbers in the past decade, it would be misleading to think that it will simply take 'one more heave' for them to move through into senior management. Women tend to move into those areas of professional and managerial employment where they may be able to exercise high levels of skill and expertise but have little effective organisational discretion. Whilst women are increasingly gaining entry to jobs demanding high levels of expertise, they are only rarely translating these into jobs with high levels of authority and organisational power . . .[4]

No change there then, as we might colloquially express it. Women, whether in the publicly visible realms of politics or less visible areas such as the City or the legal profession, have made few incursions into what is generally regarded as 'real' social power, in the sense of power which is able to enact and enforce institutional and structural change. As Gillian Youngs has argued: 'The strategy of allowing women into paid employment, but segregating them from men and paying them less has continued to grow in significance in terms of the kinds of employment involved, the geographical globalisation of the economy and its recent processes of restructuring'.[5]

But before assuming that there has been no significant change in the sex of those 'in power' (in Britain or the West generally) we need to raise two further issues. The first is the question of what constitutes social power (an issue which will be discussed in a subsequent chapter); the second, which is of concern here, involves a consideration of how we interpret the changes which clearly have taken place in gender relations and in the relationship of women and men to paid work. As we have seen, Giddens has interpreted what he sees as the democratization of intimacy as part of a shift towards a more generally democratic society. We could also interpret that shift in terms not of a move towards greater democracy but towards greater integration between the social and the personal worlds. Marx would have seen this as part of the process of commodification: the translation of all forms of social relationship into relationships dictated by the cash nexus. Weber would interpret the homogenization of male and female experience as a move towards that 'iron cage' which he predicted would be the fate of people in technologically sophisticated, 'rationalized' capitalist societies.

In assessing changes that have occurred within the lives of women in the past 40 years we thus arrive at one of the most interesting, and potentially controversial, questions related to gender and social theory. It is the question of how those manifest changes in the lives of women have actually made a substantial difference to either social theory or the social world. The entry of large numbers of women into lifelong patterns of employment is clearly personally significant, as are those changes in the extension of personal freedoms in terms of issues related to sexuality and reproduction. But how – to borrow an expression from literary criticism – should we 'read' this? Have we seen emancipation or integration? Have we seen, in the past 30 years in the West, a move to that androgynous world of George Orwell's *Nineteen Eighty-Four*, in which 'real' power is held by men, but society allows women into paid work and into an apparent form of sexual and public emancipation? Orwell's vision of the future has in many ways been denied by the actual reality of the twenty-first century (in which there is far more space for personal and social dissent than he allowed), but an aspect of his vision which remains pertinent is the emergence of androgyny and the public disappearance of the recognition of sexual difference. Scott Lash, for example, identified what he has described as 'de-differentiation' in a book published 41 years after Orwell's novel.[6]

Although separated by some 30 years, the work of George Orwell and Max Weber has much in common, for both men were deeply concerned about the creation of societies dominated by technical rationality. John

Jervis has expressed eloquently the psychological cost of modernity when
he writes that:

> Work becomes compulsive, neurotic, work for work's sake, a
> driven asceticism, an endless treadmill; in effect, a 'tradition
> without traditionalism'. The world of rational reflexive modern-
> ity again confronts its own neuroses in its denunciation of the
> irrationalities of popular culture, and its disparagement of other
> activities – like 'housework' – that actually resemble 'work' in
> precisely the 'irrationalities' so disparaged, namely, the routine,
> the fetishism, the excess of point and purpose that makes the
> whole project self-defeating.[7]

But this account of emotional and personal life in late modernity, while
accurate in itself, nevertheless essentially repeats what Weber had said in
The Protestant Ethic and the Spirit of Capitalism:

> The moral conduct of the average man was thus deprived of its
> planless and unsystematic character and subjected to a consistent
> method for conduct as a whole . . . the end of this asceticism was
> to be able to lead an alert, intelligent life: the most urgent task the
> destruction of spontaneous, impulsive enjoyment, the most import-
> ant means was to bring order into the conduct of its adherents.[8]

These ends have clearly been achieved in those workplaces described by
Arlie Hochschild (and mentioned in the previous chapter). They have also
arguably been achieved – and are being achieved – in intimate relationships, so much so that what Giddens describes as democratization might
also be described as rationalization: women and men view each other, and
their relationships with each other, less in terms of 'love' or 'romance' and
more in terms of the convenience and the suitability of the other. Here we
tread on dangerous ground, if not actually thin ice, since there is considerable historical evidence to suggest that many people have always married
for prosaic and material reasons: reasons concerning succession and the
maintenance of property and lineage for the upper class, and reasons concerning provision and effective housekeeping for the middle and working
classes. So before we move too rapidly to the assumption that modern
women and men are choosing their partners for material reasons, and
reasons of social convenience, we need to recall that this was *always* a possibility. It is clear that the revolution in sexual attitudes and behaviour in
the West in the past 30 years has changed the way in which relationships
are initiated and conducted, but this is not to suggest that we have become
any less (or more) circumspect and predictable than we were in the past
about who we marry.

Having married, or entered into a long-term relationship, we are – particularly in Britain and the USA – very likely to end the relationship prior to

death. What death and migration did to the family in the nineteenth century, divorce and separation do to it in the late twentieth and early twenty-first centuries. The countries in the West with the highest rates of female participation in the labour market are also the countries with the highest rates of divorce. Again, we are faced with one of the questions of interpretation which should preoccupy the sociologist: is this a sign of the democratization of which Giddens speaks, or of an absurdly hedonistic culture incapable of maintaining long-term relationships, or of a society in which women in particular no longer feel obligated to maintain unsatisfactory personal relationships? Giddens, Ulrick Beck and Elisabeth Gernsheim-Beck have all written about personal and intimate relations: in reviewing and assessing their work we can locate some of the questions which sociological theory now has to ask, and answer, about how women and men live their lives.[9]

During the 1970s and 80s, feminist sociologists and psychologists drew up an account of the behaviour of women and men in personal relationships which essentially proposed what has become known as – to follow the title of a popular book on the subject – the thesis of *Men are from Mars, Women are from Venus*. On both sides of the Atlantic – and indeed, from across the Channel – it was argued that women and men saw the world, and acted in it, in different ways. In both Britain and the USA feminists recognized the work of previous generations of women social scientists, and it was acknowledged that the distinct social experiences of women had been recorded. Thus the work of Miria Komarovsky (a member of the Frankfurt School) was revisited and it was remarked that Komarovsky's account of the ways in which women underperformed in scholastic tests in order to preserve conventional expectations of femininity had changed little between 1950 and 1970.[10] Betty Friedan, in *The Feminine Mystique* (1963), outlined the social and individual consequences of domestic life in the suburbs of the USA, and Hannah Gavron, in *The Captive Wife*, initiated the study (to be more fully developed by Ann Oakley) of the 'private life of the household'.[11] In these and other studies women were put on the agenda of sociology, albeit in the most minimal and marginal way.

The marginality of the study of women in the home, and women's attitude to paid work and educational success, started to change in the 1970s. In the USA, emphasis was placed on the study of women in professional and educational structures.[12] Essentially the debate was about the refusal of institutional structures, dominated by men, to allow women access. In Britain, more academic energy was diverted towards the question of the relative importance of gender and/or class in the determination of an individual woman's social experiences and life chances. Marxist feminism argued that the class relations of capitalist society were such as to segregate people by class quite as much as by gender. 'The long revolution' of the emancipation of women was not to be achieved, argued writers such as Juliet Mitchell and Sheila Rowbotham,[13] except in the context of a socialist revolution. This view – supported by evidence from state socialist societies about state responsibility for child care – suggested that the transformation of gender relations would only be possible if class relations were also transformed. Not so, argued Diana Leonard, Christine Delphy and Lisa Adkins.[14] In exchanges with Mary McIntosh and Michele Barrett, Leonard and Delphy argued that gender was a more rigid and more effective form of social segregation, and the creation of social hierarchies, than that of class: 'materialist feminism' for Leonard and Delphy meant not materialism in the Marxist sense, but a materialism which assigned sexual differentiation a primary place in the organization of the social world.

This view, as radical in its ways as Marxist feminism, depended to a certain extent on what is – and was – collectively known as 'French feminism'.[15] This term referred to a group of French feminists (Hélène Cixous, Luce Irigaray and Monique Wittig) who argued not for sexual equality but for the recognition of sexual difference. Unlike their famous predecessor in the struggle against Gallic misogyny, Simone de Beauvoir, these women had no sympathy for her praise, in the conclusion to *The Second Sex*, of modern women: 'The "modern" woman accepts masculine values: she prides herself on thinking, taking action, working, creating, on the same terms as men; instead of seeking to disparage them, she declares herself their equal'.[16] Cixous, Irigaray and Wittig had absolutely no wish to shackle themselves to the model of social equality and post-Enlightenment rationality proposed by de Beauvoir. As Hélène Cixous put it: 'By writing her self, woman will return to the body which has been more than confiscated from her, which has been turned into the uncanny stranger on display . . .'[17] Women, these feminist writers argued, are different from men: they write differently, think differently and experience the world in different ways. Femininity, and the feminine, is not to be scorned or mocked (an inevitable conclusion for many readers of *The Second Sex*), but to be celebrated. This argument was taken up by other writers such as Adrienne Rich in the USA who wrote in praise of specifically female experiences, most notably motherhood. In her book, *A Woman Born*, and the article 'Compulsory Heterosexuality', Rich argued for the recognition of the feminine and, importantly, its liberation from the capture and distortion imposed upon it by men and the masculine.[18] John Jervis has described the debates thus:

> Should women use the language of Enlightenment rationality in defending and extending their rights, at the risk of explicitly endorsing what may be masculinist notions of politics and the public sphere? Or should they use the postmodern language of 'difference', arguing that universalising norms have been insensitive to women's aspirations and rights to their own identities,

even though it is clear that, historically, 'difference' can easily slide into 'inequality' and 'inferiority', and that anyway such a strategy could fall victim to the dilemmas of 'identity politics' . . .[19]

This account gives only a brief introduction to what was, in effect, a war about gender in both the social sciences and the humanities in western universities in the 1970s. Sociology was not exempt from this, and the professional associations in both Britain and the USA were forced to put into place both special study groups for the discussion of women and institutional practices which assured women rights of participation in decision making. In this decade it was women who attacked sociology for what was seen as its refusal of women both institutionally and theoretically. What started to complicate even further this discontent with the concerns of sociology was the participation by gay people, and people of colour, in the voicing of dissatisfaction. Sociology stood accused of having refused to acknowledge, let alone study, the worlds of those people who were not white or male. It was accepted that sociology had always included the working class in its vision, but that vision had been one which had defined social exclusion or social disadvantage largely in terms of discrimination in the labour market. A new agenda and new perceptions began to challenge sociology.

This agenda – and these perceptions – emerged in part out of the new politics of the 1970s and from the theoretical innovations of Foucault, Paul Layotard *et al.*, which proposed *inter alia* new understandings of the locations and mechanisms of social power.[20] Resistance to heterosexuality, feminism and demands for civil rights for racial and ethnic minorities were hardly a new development within European or North American culture, but all these forms of political and intellectual dissent had been largely kept apart from the academy of which sociology was a part. When, from *within* the academy, new interpretations of the world emerged which offered a shift away from the prioritization of the discussion of the formal, institutional world, then new concerns could, and did, initiate academic interest. Thus, in 1981 Jeffrey Weeks rewrote the history of sexuality in Britain in a way which was explicitly informed by Foucault.[21] Paul Gilroy and Stuart Hall demonstrated the implicit racism of ideas about 'British' culture, and Edward Said (a literary critic rather than a sociologist) demonstrated the links between western culture and imperialist politics.[22] Maggie Humm, like Said, a literary critic, used the term 'border crossing' to describe the ways in which cultures absorb and integrate (but often do not acknowledge) influences.[23]

Thus, by the beginning of the 1980s sociology had recognized that its subject matter was even more eclectic than previously supposed. It became appropriate to study areas of social life previously ignored, and to study these areas with new methods and new assumptions. Liz Stanley and Sue

Wise published *Breaking Out: Feminist Consciousness and Feminist Research* in 1983, and in so doing demonstrated the emergent diversity of sociological method.[24] Stanley and Wise gave a place to the participants in research and argued for the political engagement of the researcher. If this was not the first time that this idea had been expressed within sociology (C. W. Mills' *The Sociological Imagination* explicitly endorses the idea of political transparency), it was the first time that women's ideas had been situated within the context of a specifically female process of social research.[25] The idea of 'objectivity' was found to be inadequate and wanting: it was no longer possible, it was argued, to suppose that any sociologist could offer an objective picture of the social world or a particular social process. The best that could be offered would be a convincing narrative about all aspects of social existence. In order to achieve this, sociologists had to acknowledge what Nancy Hartsock was to describe as their 'standpoint', or – as it has been put many times in classrooms across the West – an account of where the researcher is 'coming from'.[26]

In this context (and the following chapter will develop the discussion of the idea of gendered narratives in sociology), the examination of the personal, the private and the intimate by sociologists in the last 20 years of the twentieth century came to be organized around the idea of 'difference'. Black people, gays, women, transsexuals and the physically disadvantaged were no longer interpreted in terms of their difference from the ideal of white manhood, but in terms of their *particularity*. The universal subject, the assumption of the 'he' as the universal human being, began to disappear and with it, following Foucault, the idea that power is hierarchical. Foucault had disabused a generation of sociologists of the view that individuals could be located in hierarchies of social power; in Foucault's account of knowledge there was no dominant view, but competing discourses. This view gave women (at least theoretically) access to the construction and articulation of ideas, but what it diminished (as feminists have pointed out) was any recognition of the refusal of women's ideas through explicit patriarchal power.[27] Feminists have discussed at some length the implications of Foucault's work for feminism (since in empowering women and women's sexuality through an account of competing discourses, Foucault also effectively disempowers women by refusing an account of the social world which locates fixed power), but it is equally important to point out that Foucault has had a profound importance in allowing feminist historians to abandon a rigid emancipatory version of history and recognize instead the multiplicity of women's, and feminist, discourses in the past.[28]

The shift in sociology in the 1970s and 80s (through the influence of both Foucault and the politics of the decades) made gender an essential part of sociological thinking. But how – and why – is more complex than simply observing that thinking about gender is now part of the sociological curriculum. As noted above, Giddens (and others) attempted to link ideas about gender (and specifically changing ideas about gender) to theoretical accounts of society. This is not in itself a novel departure for sociology, since writers within the classic tradition (notably Marx and Weber) have long been known for their accounts of the way in which ideological changes are related to structural change. Neither Marx nor Weber specifically linked changes in ideas about gender to changes in the social structure, but both established the thesis (with different emphases) that 'ideas' (in the most general sense) are linked to the social relations, and the social organization, of any society. In the most famous sociological account of the links between ideological and structural change – *The Protestant Ethic and the Spirit of Capitalism* – Max Weber emphasizes the impact of Protestant asceticism on *men*. His comments have led subsequent generations to interpret the use of 'men' in two ways: to assume that women are somehow generally excluded from the Protestant ethic and/or to berate Weber for excluding women from his discussion. These assumptions led to the view that the 'classic' tradition in sociology ignores women. But if we look at the existing relations between women and men in the West, what we might see are not the omissions of Marx and Weber, but their relevance. In particular, what we might see is the centrality of the ideas of Marx and Weber to our present social world, whether individual or social. In using Marx and Weber to examine contemporary gender relations we might also conclude that the assumptions of the 'founding fathers' about gender are less entirely naturalistic than is often supposed.

In returning, to Marx and Weber for an understanding of the lives of individuals in the twenty-first century, we cannot expect to find ideas specifically about gender. As suggested earlier, the radicalism of Marx and Weber lay not in their specific discussion of women and men, gender or relations between gender, but in the denaturalization of the social world. Marx and Weber challenged the idea that the social world was created by 'natural' or organic processes; while they left aspects of the social world untouched by social examination (in particular the 'natural' differences between women and men) they brought all other aspects of the social world into the scope of their examination. Thus what we can take from Marx and Weber about gender – and the behaviour and values of women and men – is the idea that both women and men are capable of absorbing and integrating socially produced values into their understanding, and consequently into their behaviour. Once we accept this idea, those heterosexual couples living in 'confluent love', who exist in the pages of Giddens, become rather less the agents of the new democracy and rather more the products of an ethic of work and contract.

Once we recognize, or at least envisage, the possibility that women, just as much as men, are capable of integrating the Protestant ethic (not to mention the spirit of capitalism) into their normative world, then social theory and its relationship to feminism begins to acquire a different way of looking at the world other than that of the assumption of male power and female subordination, accompanied by a theoretical refusal of women. Moreover, the change in the social world which Giddens envisaged as a result of more democratic gender relations begins to look less like a change in the social world, and more like a greater integration of more people into the values of late capitalism. The changes that have visibly occurred in the social experience of women in the twentieth century (notably in relation to labour force participation and control of fertility) do challenge social theory, in that we have to ask what kind of impact these changes are having on the social world. Giddens has provided one answer, Marx and Weber arguably provide others, while Foucault provides still different theoretical possibilities. Giddens and Foucault both argue, albeit in different ways, that society can be changed by changing ideas about sexuality, while a reading of Marx and Weber would suggest that neither man would see capitalist society as *essentially* changed by changes in the organization of gender. For Marx and Weber, what has taken place in terms of the reorganization of gender, and relations between the genders, would indicate the capacity of capitalism and the capitalist ethic to act as an integrative force. In particular, Weber's account of bureaucratic dominance, material calculation and rationalizing pressures seems endlessly relevant to the quality of individual lives in late capitalism: this is a society in which calculative rationality dominates individual thinking and thus determines every aspect of personal life. Men have long been prisoners of the 'iron cage'; in reading Weber we can also conjecture that there is no reason to suppose that women should not similarly become imprisoned. For example, we can note (as Sylvia Walby has done) that 'Younger women who are highly educated and gain good jobs are reducing the gender gap'.[29] However, we might also note that women outside this classification fare badly in the labour market, and that while the labour market increasingly allows women access to high status, high reward jobs when they are prepared to conform to traditional male expectations, it is less pliable when traditional female expectations (in particular motherhood) are manifested.

Weber's account of the 'iron cage' is perhaps more relevant to the experience of human beings in the twenty-first century than any other account. In his essay on bureaucracy, Weber discussed the processes of bureaucratization and rationalization – processes which are as much a part of our social world today as they were at the beginning of the twentieth century. Weber's comments on the need for specialist knowledge, the proliferation of educational certificates and the construction of the authority of bureaucratic order could all be used to describe the present social order of the West. (We might also note that the discussion of bureaucracy takes place within the context of a longer discussion of 'power'.) But at the conclusion of the essay Weber asks two questions which are relevant here. The first is that of the extent to which administrative structures are subject to economic determination. The second is that of the extent to which bureaucratic structures themselves create 'economic effects'.

To illustrate this we can take the example of the bureaucratization of British universities in the 1980s and 1990s. The original impulse for the instigation of this process came from a political commitment to the expansion of higher education. (An expansion to be assessed in terms of the numbers of students within higher education.) However, that policy was generated within an ideological climate which endorsed a form of economic organization derived from the market: one of 'value for money' and 'accountability'. Thus what was put in place was a bureaucratic structure which was in part related to the economic, but organized largely through assumptions about appropriate forms of management. These forms of management had in their turn an 'economic effect' in that they created a climate in which a number of universities considered the possibility of becoming privately organized and financed institutions. In short, the imposition of a new strata of bureaucratic management (what Marilyn Strathern has referred to as the 'audit culture') led to the discussion of what is perceived as the freedom of the 'deregulated' private sphere.[30]

In this case we can see very clearly a process in which regulation by the state creates a response which demands deregulation. If we extend the argument to professions other than that of the universities we can also find examples of the call by professional groups for reorganization in structures outside the bureaucratic control of the state. Schoolteachers and doctors have been prominent among those who have spoken for this policy in contemporary Britain. Weber was entirely correct in supposing that bureaucracy would become the predominant form of social organization. But he also suggests that bureaucracy's iron grip extends beyond the world of paid work:

> Behind all the present discussions of the foundations of the educational system, the struggle of the 'specialist type of man' against the older type of 'cultivated man' is hidden at some decisive point. This fight is determined by the irresistibly expanding bureaucratization of all public and private relations of authority and by the ever-increasing importance of expert and specialised knowledge. This fight intrudes into all intimate cultural questions.[31]

In this passage there is much of interest, but in this context it is the final two sentences that are the most interesting and perhaps the most relevant. Weber's use of language (or his translator's use of language) suggests a violent encounter between different cultures, and if we consider many of the cultural changes which have occurred in the second half of the twentieth century, we can suggest examples which illuminate Weber's thesis. In particular, we can point to the changes that have occurred in sexual politics and ask whether or not the integration of women into public life (that is, not just into paid work but also into the dominant value system) has not diminished almost to the point of disappearance what were once assumed to be 'natural' differences between women and men. At the same time it is also important to recognize that Weber, writing at the beginning of the twentieth century, did not experience those postmodern shifts in the articulation of gender differences which have led John Jervis to describe the postmodern as the 'revenge of the feminine'.[32] In this account, the postmodern world becomes, at least in cultural terms, 'feminine'; the fault lines are masculine and feminine and explicitly related to gender, if not to biology. Thus if we unite these two accounts of late modernity what could be suggested is a gendered version of Weber: some women increasingly participate in 'specialist' knowledge, but 'nature' and the 'cultivated man' of which Weber speaks are increasingly represented by those who cannot achieve, or refuse, integration into a particular form of education and accredited competence. Women, as biological rather than gendered selves, do not remain outside 'specialized knowledge' but femininity – particularly if it is seen in the terms outlined by Cixous *et al.* – arguably might do so.

It is at this point that it is possible to bring together the insights of writers as diverse as Max Weber, George Orwell and Beverley Skeggs. Both Weber and Orwell foresaw the future as a world dominated by bureaucratic control; Beverley Skeggs has suggested that working-class women are concerned to maintain 'femininity' in their construction of self.[33] The link between these authors (which is not immediately apparent) is that it is possible to argue that the changes taking place in late capitalism are precisely those that Weber and Orwell predicted, but with certain specific provisos – one of the most important of which is that those women most disadvantaged by the class system (i.e. working-class women of whatever racial origin) are those least likely to seek integration into the world of specialist skills. In this, of course, we see exactly the possibility envisaged by Orwell: that outside the socially accredited and the functionaries of bureaucratic society there will be a class of people distinct from the dominant social order. Orwell described these people as 'proles'; sociologists describe them as the 'underclass'. The segmentation of the working class into the underclass and those who are gainfully employed and equipped with socially confirmed 'skills' is further associated with the disappearance of highly distinct forms of gendered behaviour, except among those who are most socially and economically disadvantaged. For working-class women, unlikely to be able to afford either higher education or child care, it is socially effective to attempt to maintain the feminine or femininity since it may offer access to male support. Equally, as Terry Lovell has pointed out, 'There is some evidence that femininity as cultural capital is beginning to have broader currency in unexpected ways'.[34]

With this remark Lovell is referring to those characteristics – such as caring, manual dexterity and relative docility – often associated with women. Women have become, in short, the ideal employees of the current form of capitalism, in which profit is generated through service and consumer-led production rather than in manufacturing industry. Thus what is sometimes hailed as 'emancipation' has to be regarded at least sceptically: the needs of the new forms of production have facilitated and encouraged the employment of women quite as much as commitments to sexual equality. Within these new worlds of work, women are allowed to share with men both the advantages and disadvantages of paid work. It would be premature to assume that either advantages or disadvantages dominate the nature of that experience. But what we can observe is that the traditional aspirations of femininity (in particular childbearing) are now being negotiated within a set of expectations which often, although not always, include the ongoing participation of women in the labour market.[35] Even so, the attitudes of women towards paid work may remain, as Catherine Hakim has controversially suggested, different to those of men.[36] Critics have attacked Hakim and argued that her work ignores factors such as the socialization of women or the limited range of employment available to women.[37] All arguments in this context are related to assumptions about the 'nature' of women (and men). Here, it is important to emphasize that both sides of the argument about women and paid work often overlook the power of the social world to create and mould our behaviour – a factor which both Marx and Weber were very much more prepared to recognize than some contemporary critics. Equally, while there is furious debate about the meaning of paid work to women, there is also intense debate about the political strategies necessary to minimize social inequality. That political debate – about the politics of recognition and the politics of redistribution – is now a central part of social theory. But first, it is necessary to establish the meaning of the self – the person – in social theory. In part that debate depends upon our understanding of the person – the self – at the centre of social theory. John Holmwood and Andrew Sayer have returned to the question of the relationship between capitalism and patriarchy, and in their exchanges Andrew Sayer has raised the crucial issue of whether 'men and women have to live in the gendered ways we know?'[38] The construction of those 'men and women' of the social world is the subject of the next chapter.

CHAPTER **4**

THE GENDERED SELF

One of the ideas that has been established firmly by academic feminism is that the 'self', the human being at the centre of both political and social theory, was until recently umproblematically male. It is perhaps an exaggeration to say that there was no challenge to this view until second-wave feminism (Mary Wollstonecraft and John Stuart had intervened in the debate in the eighteenth and nineteenth centuries, but it is possible to say that in general there was little public discussion or criticism of the assumption of the male citizen until the 1970s). The great statements about the organization of the West – from the Declaration of Independence to the Beveridge Report – assumed that men were the citizens and that women existed, if at all, in a region outside political discourse. The social contract of the West, as Carole Pateman pointed out, was deeply gendered.[1] It was within this gendered culture that sociology was established, and the deconstruction of the gender of the citizen was one (if not the essential) aim of academic feminism. Sociology, in common with all other academic subjects, stood accused of basing its theoretical tradition upon a naturalistic account of the social world, an account which assumed a given 'nature' and social role for men and women.

It was thus that in the 1970s feminist academics within the social sciences took issue with the implicit gendering of the human subject. Carole Pateman and Jean Elshtain in political science, Irene Bruegel, Veronica Beechey and Susan Himmelweit in economics and Ann Oakley, Sheila Allen and Margaret Stacey in sociology were just a few of a generation which looked at academic disciplines and found them lacking in both the explicit discussion of women and in an understanding and recognition of the implications of theoretical statements made on the basis of the assumption that a citizen (or a paid worker) was male.[2] Pateman (and others) argued that 'traditional' (that is pre-second wave) theory was mistaken in its conclusions because it did not recognize gender difference. This bold claim asserted that the 'gendering' of theory would not just add to the range of social experience discussed, but would alter the theoretical frameworks through which we see the world. The argument therefore took one step further the claim by Simone de Beauvoir in *The Second Sex* that woman was 'the other', suggesting that not only was woman 'the other' but an other whose exclusion led to false theoretical claims.[3] While de Beauvoir had assumed that the problem for social theories about women was women's exclusion from them, second-wave feminism took the step – which de Beauvoir had not – of questioning the validity of post-Enlightenment social and political theory.

The literature on de Beauvoir has now become extensive and a consensus has emerged within it that she was a far more original philosopher than previously supposed and that her analysis of the position of women in the twentieth century is more challenging to male assumptions than previously thought. Toril Moi, Sonia Kruks, Judith Butler and Vikki Bell have all argued, albeit with different emphases, that it is incorrect to see de Beauvoir as a woman claiming entry to a male world of rationality, and rather more appropriate to see her as a major contributor to the debate about women and agency.[4] The most important initial statement in the debate is de Beauvoir's own remark in *The Second Sex* which asserts that 'one is not born a woman: one becomes one'.[5] This remark can be appropriated by different theoretical viewpoints: by those who argue that we acquire our gendered selves through socialization (which elaborates a biologically given self) and by those who argue that sexual difference is entirely constructed and that we construct our gendered selves through 'performativity' – the 'performance' of socially established expectations of the masculine or the feminine. As Sonia Kruks has pointed out: 'This paradoxical quality of selfhood is captured in Beauvoir's notion of "becoming" a woman: "to become" can mean to undergo a process of change or formation; and it can also mean to alter oneself. "Becoming" a woman means both'.[6]

In the first camp would be those who accept the givens of biology, while in the second would be those (and most influentially Judith Butler) who argue that all gendered behaviour is a matter of the internalization of social expectations. As must be apparent, what is at issue here is an ancient debate about nature and nurture, but a debate made more intense and more furious by twentieth-century advances in the technological control of reproduction and the consequent diminution of the impact of the 'natural' on the social experience of women and men. We can now live, at least in the West, within a world in which the impact of biological difference upon our physical lives can be radically eliminated, if not ignored altogether. (The question of the elimination of the impact of biological difference upon our emotional lives, and our imagination, remains more contentious.)

It was to this world that Judith Butler addressed her most influential work, *Gender Trouble*, in 1990.[7] The book is not specifically about women (although feminist literature and feminism figure centrally in its consideration) and it has been integrated into debates across the social sciences about the ways we construct our biology. *Gender Trouble* argues that gender is acquired rather than given, that women and men elaborate expectations of femininity and masculinity and that gender (or more accurately the correct display of gender) is crucial to social cohesion and social order. In *Gender Trouble* (and in her later work, *Bodies that Matter*) Butler is at pains to stress the social coercion implicit (and often explicit) within social expectations about appropriate gender behaviour. In effect, what Butler challenges is a long-lasting tradition which assumes that although there may be differences (across time and cultures) between the masculine and the feminine, there is always a social interplay with an existing, 'natural', sexed being. Butler rejects this assumption and argues that there is no 'male' or 'female' person on which a particular script of sexually appropriate behaviour is imposed.

The radical challenge of Butler's work to the cultural and social world of the West (indeed the entire planet) has not been overlooked. Part of its appeal lies in the possibilities for the discussion of themes across the social sciences and the humanities. Butler can thus be used to study not just, let us say, the ways in which adolescents 'do' gender, but equally the way in which writers of fiction construct their plots and their characters in order, Butler would ague, to secure fixed gendered behaviour. Not for Butler debates about agendas of homosexuality: for her all such debates (and discussion about any sexual identity whether heterosexual, transsexual or homosexual) are premised on fundamentally incorrect understandings (in particular dichotomous expectations about the difference between male and female) and serve only to preserve expectations about sexual difference. Moreover, rather than reject Freud and the tradition of psychoanalysis, Butler turns him (and his followers) into allies through an emphasis on Freud's articulation of the unstable, insecure human being of actual existence. Ideals of masculinity and femininity are, for Butler, constructed in order to secure social order rather than evolving, changing cultural patterns which have built on 'natural' distinctions and divisions:

> The deconstruction of identity is not the deconstruction of politics; rather, it establishes as political the very terms through which identity is articulated. This kind of critique brings into question the foundationalist frame in which feminism as an identity politics has been articulated. The internal paradox of this foundationalism is that it presumes, fixes and constrains the very 'subjects' that it hopes to liberate.[8]

In looking at the social world through the eyes of Judith Butler we can see a gendered organization which certainly does play a central part in the maintenance of social cohesion across all cultures. Whether a society is one of technologically sophisticated late capitalism or a hunting and gathering society, Butler would argue that gender differentiation is central to social organization and a major form of differential access to social power. In the twentieth-century West, coercion – until the period after the Second World War – had been directed towards the maintenance of heterosexuality as the dominant mode of adult behaviour. The sexual liberalization of the 1970s marked, for Butler, a movement towards the recognition of different forms of sexuality but nevertheless still maintained the dominance of heterosexuality, since homosexuality maintained its status as a practice defined by its difference from heterosexuality rather than being distinct in itself. Butler's politics are explicitly directed towards the recognition of the coercive within expectations about sexuality and demand the disappearance of what she describes as 'the very binarism of sex and . . . its fundamental unnaturalness'.[9] The implications of this idea, while acceptable as a strategy in issues related to sexuality are, for many writers, less acceptable when directed towards instances of specific forms of discrimination built on gendered expectations.

The most fully argued opposition to Judith Butler on this point has come from two of her fellow citizens: Nancy Fraser and Martha Nussbawm.[10] Both have taken Butler to task for what they see as her absence of understanding of the material in the determination of individual life chances. Fraser, writing in an exchange with Judith Butler, argued that:

> Thus we can now answer one of the questions posed earlier: the economic disabilities of homosexuals are better understood as effects of heterosexism in the relations of recognition than as hardwired in the structure of capitalism. The good news is that we do not need to overthrow capitalism in order to remedy those disabilities – although we may well need to overthrow it for other reasons. The bad news is that we need to transform the existing status order and restructure the relations of recognition.[11]

To this accusation Butler did not reply by rejecting the importance of the material. On the contrary, her argument is that it is through the construction of masculinity and femininity that a great deal of material social inequality is maintained. In a paper written before the publication of *Gender Trouble*, Mike Brake had used the title 'I may be queer, but at least I'm a man' to discuss the ways in which the social system of the West has a hierarchy of gender differentiation and identity.[12] At the most powerful point in the hierarchy are white, middle-class, heterosexual males, while at the least powerful point might be black (or non-white), working-class lesbians. Brake thus recognized that sexual identity plays a part in the construction of a powerful social identity, but unlike Butler he does not argue that it is sexual identity which is the crucial determinant of our social power and prestige. Butler would argue (indeed, in the exchange with Fraser

she does argue) that she is not unaware of the differences in material circumstances between individuals. But what she wants to bring to our attention – and here she performs a crucially important task for social scientists
– is the extent to which the social world is suffused with questions and
decisions about sexual identity. Thus 'doing' gender, as we might conceptu-
alize it at the beginning of the twenty-first century, is very far from a simple
demonstration of our 'natural' biology.

So far, so good, for many social scientists, literary critics and historians.
In the years after Foucault deconstructed the idea of hierarchical power and
the relations of power there were very few writers in either the social sciences or the humanities who were not aware of the diversity of human
experience and (since that was always the case) the theoretical implications
of the acceptance of that idea, of which the most important aspect was the
recognition of multiple sites of power. Post-Foucault, it is impossible not
to recognize, and to acknowledge, the diverse forms of human existence
and human experience and their interdependence. For example, we have
to recognize that conventional heterosexuality is actually premised on the
rejection of sexual relations with people of the same sex: the homosexual
presence at the centre of all heterosexual relationships is not made explicit,
but underpins all those single-sex activities which in effect maintain the
possibility of heterosexuality. Thus, single-sex institutions (or patterns of
behaviour) in effect have as their central function the maintenance of sexual
difference. Neither Fraser or Nussbawm would disagree with the social
importance of those institutions which are organized around sexual difference. But where they do take issue with Butler and other theorists who
might generally be described as the prophets of the sexual (rather than the
social) world, is on the issue of politics and the validity of legal and social
protest about inequalities between women and men.

This debate relates clearly to the recent work of Judith Butler, *Excitable
Speech: A Politics of the Performative*, but it also has a longer history and
wider implications.[13] In *Excitable Speech*, Butler takes issue with legal pro-
hibitions in the USA of 'hate speech' and pornography (comparable legislation exists throughout Europe). She argues that such legislation is problematic
because the legal system disempowers those who might resist for themselves – that is, the law takes away from individual human beings opportunities for protest and dissent. Far from maintaining a 'free' society, legislation
against specific forms of representation actually diminishes freedom. For
example, if we know that there is a law against, let us say, the incitement to
racial hatred, then we are, according to Butler, more likely to cite the law
than to take issue with the source of the specific prejudice. Butler does not
spell out all the implications of her position, but her thesis suggests that
state legislation against forms of prejudice and discrimination produces
both an intellectual and a social laziness in individuals as well as a politics
of state rather than of individual responsibility.

It is possible to challenge Butler – as, indeed Martha Nussbawm has done – by aligning her with libertarianism, and right-wing libertarianism at that. In this vein, Nussbawm has argued that:

> Butler's argument has implications well beyond the cases of hate speech and pornography. It would appear to support not just quietism in these areas, but a much more general legal quietism – or, indeed, a radical libertarianism. It goes like this: let us do away with everything from building codes to non-discrimination laws to rape laws because they close the space within which the injured tenants, the victims of discrimination, the raped women, can perform their resistance.[14]

Resistance, as Nussbawm goes on to point out, is pivotal for Butler, and thus any process or institution which seems to inhibit it is to be dismissed or regarded with great suspicion. It is not just that Butler fears that state intervention is an assault on individual liberty, but that what is maintained through state intervention is the prescriptive regime of sexuality and gender performance which she sees as maintaining pornography and discourses of sexual confrontation.

Debates about Judith Butler's work will no doubt persist for some time, not least because it has given rise to ways of thinking (not to mention ways of being) which have become influential in the western academy. But if we stand back from the debates and away from engagement or commitment with any particular participant, what can be seen is an intellectual reaction (indeed resistance) to the pressures of conformity in late capitalism. Butler, particularly in *Excitable Speech*, is essentially arguing for spontaneity and against institutionalization – an argument which is familiar territory to readers of Weber or Simmel. Part of the irony of Judith Butler's work is that while she clearly wishes for the diminution of gender difference and gendered social differentiation, she also implicitly speaks *for* it: without gender difference there is no resistance, because there is no difference to resist. In the West of the twenty-first century there is a very broad church of those who would resist prejudice and discrimination against non-heterosexual people, a church which would include the woolliest of liberals with the most vocal gay activist. But the very fact of the existence (and general, although not absolute, toleration) of this alliance should suggest to us that late capitalism is barely threatened by sexual politics. The position of Butler *et al.* has always in part depended upon the idea that sexuality, and sexual politics, in some sense *matter* to capitalist social relations. At the beginning of the twenty-first century we have to entertain the idea that sexual politics, and our sexuality, may matter to us as individuals but rather less to society as a whole. The word 'society' is, of course, an abstraction (and one whose very existence has been challenged) but it is the world in which we gain our material subsistence and acquire the skills which make our social participation possible. It is very much the case that there are differences in earnings and access to public institutional power between women and men but these differences largely depend upon, and are related to, an aspect of the social world barely considered by Judith Butler – that of maternity and motherhood. Science may have created new forms of reproduction, but so far it has failed to offer a form of child care unchanged for centuries and across cultures: the primary care of children by women.

It would be wrong to claim that social theorists have always taken for granted the idea that women will care for children, the sick and the elderly. Marx, as we have seen, saw the implications of this assumption and radically challenged its continuation through his insistence on the ideological permeability of all areas of social life and his commitment to the emancipation of women via their increased participation in public production. Similarly, Weber and Simmel saw that it was impossible for individuals of either sex to live in any social world and not share the experience of exposure to its values and norms. None of these men accepted the distinction between the public and private world as one which kept women away from an understanding of the same social world as the one inhabited by men. The discussion of this issue of the gendered relationship to the public and private is crucial for social theory, since unless we engage with this debate it is all too easy to assume – as some radical feminists have done – that women occupy a different social space from that of men, both in terms of understanding and of experience. Thus, for example, the empirical evidence from all western societies that, for much of the twentieth century, women with children were absent from the labour market, was read as evidence that these women occupied a social space which was *qualitatively* different from that of men.

In the sense of the different forms of participation in everyday life, this assumption was correct. Adult women throughout the West – until the revolution in assumptions and practices about employment for women – who stayed 'at home' *did* perform the major part of household tasks and child care (a pattern not significantly changed by women's increased labour market participation rates).[15] But what is problematic are the deductions that are made from this. For those who assume that this pattern, because it is traditional, is also 'natural', there is little to explain. Women with children stay 'at home' because they choose to do so and because their aims and aspirations are different from those of men. (Catherine Hakim, in the context of evidence about women and employment, has made this point about women in Britain, and has been much attacked for doing so.)[16] For other writers on the subject (be they sociologists or political scientists) the 'fact' of women's responsibility for domestic tasks and child care is a result of deliberate or unvoiced prejudice concerning the sexual division of labour. As ever, there is a long history to this debate both in Britain and the USA. In Britain, Jane Humphries has demonstrated the ways in which early industrialization made few distinctions between women and men (or, indeed children).[17] Women and men were both allowed to work in the appalling conditions of early industrialization and those who campaigned for protective legislation and exclusionary practices often did so out of a commitment to keep women out of the worst excesses of the new factory system.

It was during this period of industrialization (the first half of the nineteenth century for Britain and later in that same century in the USA) that many attitudes and ideas about the relationship of women and men to paid work, which still inform our thinking, were developed. Two ideas became particularly significant: the idea of the 'family wage' (essentially that men should be paid enough to support their wives and children), and the belief that women were unsuited to certain kinds of employment – for example, those involving either professional skills or managerial authority.[18] Middle-class women on both sides of the Atlantic challenged the first idea at the end of the nineteenth century (and hence gained access to higher education), but the latter has remained largely unshaken and undisturbed. In periods of national crisis (notably the First and Second World Wars) women in Britain and the USA were either conscripted into or persuaded to volunteer for paid work, but this did not lead to the radical emancipation of women which is sometimes supposed. As Penny Sommerfield has concluded, 'the implementation of official policy during the war did little to alter but rather reinforced the unequal position of women in society'.[19] Moreover (and again in contradiction to some general assumptions): 'Women were not expelled from paid work after the war. They were drawn into it along lines which followed the pre-war pattern'.[20]

Britain, the Soviet Union and the USA, with their wartime rhetoric of universal involvement in the war against Germany and Japan, established a sense during those years of the possibility of shared values for women and men. The rhetoric about women and the Second World War in Britain, the Soviet Union and the USA thus differed markedly between those countries and Italy and Germany, where women as women were assigned a special – and by implication different – place in wartime rhetoric. Particularly in Germany, that place was the home and the nursery. Nazi Germany in peacetime had excluded women from the public world, except as symbols of the fertility of the nation.[21] This very different attitude to women suggests that western societies are capable of highly differentiated constructions of masculinity and femininity, and that social theorists would be wise not to assume that every western society makes the same set of assumptions about women and men and their relationship to the social world. Following Butler, however, it is important to note that although societies differ in the patterns of masculinity and femininity which they accept (and these differences are as much within society across historical periods as between societies) there are no western (or indeed other) societies which have not articulated and enforced social differences between the sexes.

However, what we can see as having evolved in Britain and USA in the years after the Second World War (the years of 'domestication' as they are sometimes described) is a continuation in both societies of the idea that women are part of the normative structure of the society, while at the same time having 'different' qualities and assumptions from those of men. Thus, contemporary western culture assumes that on the whole women and men share democratic values but that their forms of participation in the social and political world are different. Across all western societies we can observe political patterns in which men and women clearly share political and social values and also dramatically disagree. Much has been made recently of the reported tendency of women to vote for marginally more left-wing governments than men: the 'gender gap' in politics is assumed to be a fact of the present political map.[22] But it is important to remember that there was *always* a gender gap: writers on politics in the 1960s in Britain observed that women were more likely to vote for the Conservative party than men.[23] Thirty years later, the gender gap is still there, but has a different pattern to it. Explanations for this gap generally include women's concern about public services and the views of male politicians on subjects such as abortion and child care. What is evident is that women – for a number of reasons – now have to view the state more critically than in previous years. The collapse of secure forms of male employment, women's own desire to be in paid work and a culture which assumes the right of women to self-determination about fertility, combine to create a world in which many women have come to see the state as an important ally in the creation of a 'good life'.

In contemporary politics in the West there is, therefore, evidence of the impact of the different social experiences of women on their political values and ambitions. This shift has occurred at the same time as a shift in the nature of the labour market: traditional (male dominated) manufacturing industries have disappeared and new forms of employment, related in particular to the new technology and service sectors, have evolved to which large numbers of women are recruited. The professional and senior managerial middle class has remained largely untouched by gendered shifts in employment (more women enter medical schools and legal training for example, but female participation rates are considerably lower than those of men) while for a large sector of white-collar workers, paid work has become both more insecure and less regulated.[24] Therefore, new forms of clerical/supervisory employment can favour women rather than men, in that the skills related to these forms of employment may be more traditionally associated with women. *But,* and it is a very important but, significant power and material reward in the 'new' economy remain largely (as Linda McDowell has pointed out) in male hands.[25]

We can view the changes in western patterns of employment in various ways: as the result of the shift of capitalist countries from manufacturing to service industries; as evidence of the increasing pauperization and insecurity of all workers; or as evidence of the growing economic emancipation of women. In all western countries more women are in employment that at any previous time in history; in all these countries the majority of women workers are in part-time work and earn about a fifth less than men in comparable employment. But to those generations of women who left school or higher education in the 1970s, some form of paid work has become a standard expectation, not just of the period in individual lives which pre-cedes the birth of children, but of a lifetime. The number of women who remain *entirely* out of the workforce after the birth of children has become very small. Again, there is an emancipatory interpretation to this shift in employment patterns, one that suggests that women have fought against various forms of discrimination to gain entry to the labour market and would remain in the labour market throughout their lives if child care arrangements could be changed.

This argument has been highly influential with social scientists and social democratic governments. It is assumed that women wish to enter, and re-main in, employment on the same terms as men, and that public policies should be geared to make this possible. Declining birth rates throughout Europe equally suggest that where contraception and paid employment are both available, then women will choose to limit their fertility, at least in part, in order to stay in paid employment. An argument which is less often put is that in the twenty-first century, levels of economic aspiration and consumption are such that few households can maintain what is seen as an acceptable lifestyle *without* two incomes.[26] For women to be employed is not, therefore, quite so straightforwardly about emancipation and economic autonomy as is sometimes supposed. Making those arguments, however, is politically perilous, since it seems to suggest that women are in some sense abandoning their 'natural' inclinations in order to pursue material ends. This argument – the choice of money rather than children – has existed for decades: in 1942 Richard Titmuss argued that women would refuse to have children unless state services were improved; and A.J.P. Taylor described the fall of the British birth rate in the 1930s as a choice of 'a Baby Austin rather than a baby in a pram'.[27]

Without endorsing the explanations of falling birth rates offered by Titmuss and Taylor it remains important to emphasize that women's choices about fertility and participation in the labour market are often very far from 'free' and that aspirations and expectations about paid employment are too often taken from middle-class employment which offers at least a degree of job satisfaction and material reward. A number of social scientists writing about the USA have been rather quicker to point out the material demands on women than their counterparts in Britain: Barbara Ehrenreich and Richard Sennett suggested that being employed in late capitalism entirely fulfils Marx's idea of 'alienated' labour, and that it is economic constraint rather than a discourse about emancipation which underpins the participation of women with children in the labour market.[28] But in all these arguments, one consistent feature is clear: women and children are bracketed together in a way which men and children are not. We do not – in social policy or social theory – speak about the impact of unemployment on women as we might for men, or assume that special arrangements have to be made for men to enter the labour market. To all intents and purposes the labour market is governed by the expectations of men: central to which is the expectation that their children will be cared for, during the time that they are 'at work', by women. Deconstructing this idea, by arguments which suggest that women with children 'want' to be at work, has only been possible when two factors have been forgotten: that much work which many people do is boring, repetitive, insecure and not materially well rewarded, and that the need to be in paid work is not (and has never been) about personal fulfilment but about economic survival.

The labour market which women have entered in the past 20 years is one which is increasingly insecure, non-unionized and based on competition for credentials.[29] In Britain Mrs Thatcher's government did much to marginalize or eliminate trade unions from workplace regulation and thus many workers are today covered by national laws which relate to work and individual conduct within it – for example, in terms of sexual harassment – but by fewer specific workplace, or work specific, agreements. In the service industries in Britain and the USA, trade union membership is often low or non-existent, as is the job protection offered to women employed on a piece rate in seasonal or home-based work. Anne Phizacklea, Carol Wolkowitz and Sally Westwood have documented the experiences of women working in badly paid employment: this work is far from the ideal of 'having it all' or the workplace experiences of the heroines of television or films.[30] It is evident from the material collected by Phizacklea and others that many women are exploited within paid work precisely *because* of their domestic commitments: having to work at home or on domestically convenient shift work condemns them to badly paid, low-status work. Thus the contemporary regulation of the labour market suggests a concern with the regulation of the 'culture' of work rather than with the safety or material rewards of the work. In this, what could be argued (again to return to the debates between Butler, Fraser and Nussbawm) is that the material interests of all workers have sometimes been ill served by a sexualized (and gender aware) culture, in that not only have normative expectations about heterosexuality been reinforced, but this has encouraged the marginalization of material concerns.

It is here that we confront, at its most brutal, the intersection of gender and inequality. Judith Butler has argued for practices which allow individuals, essentially, to choose their gender, or the characteristics of particular genders which they wish to replicate. For childless, professionally qualified people of both sexes this practice – like that of Giddens' confluent love – is perfectly possible, and the social world can be very clearly seen to be at fault if it does not accept the talents of a woman in the same way as those of a man. But for people – and particularly female people – with children and without professional qualifications (the least favoured human beings of late capitalism) this possibility is distant. Social observation as well as shelves of books and learned documents attest to what Nancy Chodorow has called the 'reproduction of mothering' – essentially the unbroken repetition, from one generation to the next, of a social pattern in which women 'mother' and through which girls and boys learn what they perceive to be appropriate adult roles in relation to children.[31] Judith Butler may well suggest that none of us is a man or a woman in 'a seamless way' but in certain situations and certain contexts the identity of men and women is very firmly linked to their biology. Becoming a mother is one such example. Again, Butler (and others) can argue that today motherhood can be achieved and practised in different ways, but the general experience of human beings across history and across cultures is that motherhood, however differently constructed, is a condition experienced by women rather than men.[32]

This crucial instance of the relationship of gender to social life remains central to all discussions of social theory. There is little or no evidence to suggest that women who are mothers cannot, on occasion, behave as brutally or as callously as any man who is a father. Motherhood is not a moral condition, but a social one, and it is a condition experienced by the majority of the female population. As such, it has a decisive impact on women's participation in the social and political world. But in attempting to change the nature of that participation, both social theory and social policy have become involved in complex difficulties about the question of nature and gender. Some of those difficulties have been suggested above, but here it is important to bring together some of the problems with the arguments.

First, we must note the consistent contradiction underlying those arguments about women and paid work which are couched in an emancipatory discourse: arguments which assume that entry into paid work is in itself an 'emancipation'. (This argument has been made by both feminists and socialists.) Second, we need to place paid work within a specific form of political economy – that of late capitalism, a form of production which is geared to maintaining the rate of profit through individual consumption. In this society, everyone (man, woman and child) needs to play their part in consumption. But in order to do this, we must all play our part in production, since otherwise we cannot consume. Women, as much as men, are integrated into consumption through primary needs (for subsistence) and through all those constructed secondary needs of consumer choice and inclination. To try and separate the construction of gender – or the choice of gender – from this social world is impossible: gender, even if not a social given, is certainly constructed in social ways, and the 'social' is both cultural and material.

That assertion, that the social world in which we live is not just a complex, modern culture, but also a *material* world of structured (and consistent) material inequality, flies in the face of many current arguments within social and feminist theory. 'Culture' is often taken to be the defining condition of late capitalism, and social evidence about an increasing apparent 'classlessness' in culture, particularly popular culture, can seem to bear this out. Yet against this, social evidence about health, life expectancy and rates of entry to higher education all suggest that throughout the West class remains as significant as it ever was in indicating and defining what are known as 'life chances'. Women's relationship to the class structure, and its patterns of social inequality, remains complex. On the one hand the feminine (and women remain the primary location of the feminine) has been equated with modernity and modernization. On the other hand, women generally have to minimize their relationship to that most significant form of femininity, motherhood, in order to maximize their integration into modernity. In this sense, therefore, the culture both gives to women (in that there is undeniably considerable available cultural space for them) but also takes away (in that the economic market operates a significant degree of control over motherhood and over the evaluation of paid work associated with women's traditional role of 'caring').

Given these contradictions, social theory (whether by Giddens or Butler) then turns to the possibility of androgyny: if the social world can abandon 'men' and 'women' in favour of 'people', the argument goes, then these contradictions will disappear, as will the economic inequalities which arise from gender. At the beginning of the twenty-first century there is scope, in the West, for supposing that we can end the absolute link between women and childrearing. That shift may very well then diminish aspects of social inequality between women and men (to use terms which will presumably be abandoned) but the grounds for supposing that all forms of social inequality will disappear remain less secure. In conclusion, therefore, it is necessary to raise the question of the extent to which gender is *the* major form of social disadvantage. While women may generally earn, for example, less than men, this generalization obscures much similarity in pay (and rewards) between many women and men. 'Gendering' ourselves may not, in itself, involve greater or lesser social rewards, but gendering ourselves in class-specific ways emphatically does.

It is thus that Judith Butler's wish for the abandonment of 'doing gender' supposes a social vacuum. 'Doing gender' and 'doing class' are not the same thing, even if they are closely linked. As Beverley Skeggs has pointed out in her study of working-class women:

> Class was completely central to the lives of women. It was not only structural, in the sense that the division of labour organised what economic opportunities were available for them, or

institutional, in that the education was designed on this basis and operated to allocate them into this unequal division of labour, but also operated through a multitude of operations of capital transformations and trading.[33]

Following Skeggs, the question for all those concerned with social theory and its relationship to gender remains that of the extent to which theories of society (as opposed to theories about social relations) are significantly changed or altered by the discussion of gender. At the beginning of the twenty-first century it would increasingly appear that theories which see society in terms of a capitalist mode of production are left relatively unscathed by the inclusion of gender: capitalism, a consensus suggests, is gender-blind. On the other hand, theories of society which describe the social world in terms of modernity (even 'late' modernity, or 'post' modernity) are much more inclined to be posited around the centrality of gender, and gender relations, to the social world. Faced with a choice between what are, essentially, two different theoretical models (one cultural, the other material/economic) sociologists could agree to differ (which has the virtue of transparency) or to ask more questions; and in particular the question of who – and what – dominates the agenda of the twenty-first century. Notwithstanding everything that Foucault and his followers have said, there are some discourses which, if not more powerful in themselves, at least have more power attached to them. The capitalist imperative of the maintenance of profit might be used as one example here.

But the 'cultural turn' in sociology has persuaded many people that social life is now organized and regulated through culture. Yet this argument raises two questions: the first is the long-standing debate about the origin and the determinants of culture. Throughout the twentieth century, critics in the social sciences and the humanities have taken radically different positions about the fundamental question of the determinants of ideas. Marx and Engels' famous comment that 'The mode of production of material life conditions social, political and intellectual life processes in general' has been accepted in its entirety, while others have argued that Marx's account of the relationship between social ideas and social structure is far more complex than one epigrammatic statement suggests.[34] Literary critics have, in many ways, been more prepared to confront this question than sociologists, and Raymond Williams and Terry Eagleton confronted the meaning and the lived experience of class with a vigour that might cause many postmodernists to faint.[35] Indeed, English women writers of fiction, writing in often middle-class and secluded environments, have confronted the power of social class to shape individual lives and individual personalities with an energy that is seldom matched in sociology.

The second point that needs to be made here is that of the question of the extent to which sociology has increasingly become less a critical discipline and more an aspect of the dominant ideas – or at least the dominant culture – of twentieth-century society. Thus the feminist sociology which emerged in the 1970s could be interpreted not as a critical challenge to a particular understanding of the world so much as an attempt to achieve incorporation within it. Sociology – like other academic disciplines – did not warmly welcome feminists in its more disciplinary practices and institutions, but on the other hand accommodation and integration was achieved. This then raises (again) the truly problematic issue of the difference that women's participation in sociology (or for that matter any academic discipline) actually makes. Feminist sociology has significantly altered aspects of the subject matter of sociology, but the question remains as to whether this is a shift of content rather than form.

In favour of the radicalizing and transforming impact of women on sociology would be those who see, as argued in the collection of essays *Destabilizing Theory*, that feminism has brought to the academy new ways of seeing.[36] Nevertheless, *interrupting* the great tradition (be it in sociology, literary criticism or any other academic discipline) requires complex negotiations with the existing theoretical world. For example, we may agree with Skeggs that class is central to the lives of women, or with Andrew Sayer (when he writes that 'my own view is that gender orders have a fundamental affect on individuals' life chances and experience, probably affecting them more fundamentally than their class position').[37] But whichever of these two positions we find more acceptable, what remains is the social world itself. It is not to deprive women of agency to recognize that social structures may be more powerful than individual choices, and that in assessing the role of gender in the determination of life chances we find it difficult to distinguish between subjective expectations about experiences (what we might wish to be available for ourselves and others) and the objective (what is available and what others – despite our values – might wish for themselves). The 'ghost in the machine' of the contemporary world is, as ever, the human subject: acted upon and acting, but not necessarily (and often happily) conforming to social expectations, not least of sociologists. Both sociology and academic feminism have, at times, been informed by normative assumptions about human existence, not least about the attractions and desirability of the status of the rational post-Enlightenment person. Yet the great narratives of that world all recognized not just one aspect of the social world, but three: the social world itself, gender and class. Abandoning any one of those constituents of lived experience – and in particular the equation of the cultural with the social – diminishes the strength of explanation.

CHAPTER 5

THE REAL WORLD

Unkind critics of academics would suggest that it is typical of them that the 'real' world appears relatively late in a discussion about social theory and social experience. The justification for the late arrival of the 'real' world is that there seemed much to do in defining the ways in which gender is currently understood before embarking on a discussion of the reality of life in the twenty-first century. That life, for most citizens of the West, is one which is lived at a time of unparalleled domestic peace. Nevertheless, national and ethnic conflict is still endemic, and the attack on the World Trade Centre on 11 September 2001 brought home to many people in the West a new meaning of globalization. In the last decade of the twentieth century, Europe saw the outbreak of armed hostilities in the Balkans, and conflict between Israel and Palestine remains ceaseless and bitter. Globalization has not brought global peace, even though the involvement of citizens of western countries in war has become increasingly rare.

Social theory in the past 50 years has therefore had to confront both recent traumatic events as well as the more distant Holocaust and the Second World War. The major theoretical legacy of the Holocaust, as far as the social sciences is concerned, is the thesis, most fully and coherently argued by Zygmunt Baumann, that the Holocaust is 'primarily intelligible as a product of modernity.'[1] John Jervis has suggested that:

> The claim that the Holocaust is intelligible as a product of modernity – made most effectively in Baumann's work – is the claim that the characteristic modes of organisation of the modern world, and the accompanying attitudes, are entirely consistent with what we know of the Holocaust: in particular, the applied technology of mass production is the same as the applied technology of mass destruction. That modern bureaucracy

could well entail danger had been foreseen by Weber, along with the political context in which the dangers would be more likely to be realised: 'the great state and the mass party are the classic soil of bureaucratisation', he wrote, and this would lead to a 'dictatorship of the official'.[2]

According to Baumann, the modern world in which we live is one whose very values lead us not to understanding and toleration, but to authoritarianism and the systematic elimination of difference. Baumann has been widely influential, although, as Jervis remarks, it remains crucial to distinguish between the Enlightenment and modernity:

> The project of modernity entails the appropriation and transformation of the world under the aegis of instrumental reason, through a combination of technical mastery and organisational sophistication, and of the self-disciplined structure of personhood necessary to 'carry' this orientation. In this schema, no ends are absolute save that of the reproduction of that very orientation itself. Enlightenment, on the other hand, refers to the goal, the possibility of realising a community of citizenship and the social institutions and values required to maintain it. The problems arise as soon as it is realised that Enlightenment *as a project* must entail a close connection with modernity as project, and that the very attempt to constitute citizens as such will inevitably raise questions about power and its consequences . . .[3]

The literature on the Enlightenment, and on modernity, is now considerable. But if we begin to examine this literature in terms of questions about gender, and both the gender of nature and the nature of gender, what we find is a limited discussion about the intersection of gender and the Enlightenment and still less on the question of the difference (if any) that thinking about gender and the Enlightenment can make. On the issue of gender and modernity the literature is more considerable, in part because of the work which has now been produced on the feminization of culture in the early twentieth century and the establishment of close links between the 'modern' culture of the West (essentially that of the twentieth century) and the feminine. Ann Douglas, Elaine Showalter and Alice Jardine have in varied ways suggested that women claimed a place in 'modern' culture which had a transforming impact upon it, and contributed both to the denaturalization of gender and the feminization of culture.[4] Collectively, these critics argued that what occurred at the end of the nineteenth and the beginning of the twentieth centuries was a denaturalization of gender. Partly as a result of the intellectual influence of Freud and psychoanalysis, and partly because human experience began to be less immediately controlled by 'nature' and the 'natural', it began to be possible to disturb conventional assumptions about masculinity and femininity. Within this literary tradition the most important work was Virginia Woolf's *Orlando*, a discussion of the possibilities of the fluidity and variety of gender.[5] The novel is a central text in any consideration of the relationship between gender and modernity, because what Woolf proposed as gender was an idea which is as apposite to the study of the social world as it is to the literary imagination – namely, that gender is both constructed by, and constructs, the circumstances of the human subject. In her own life Woolf demonstrated her passionate hatred of fixed categories of male and female: *A Room of One's Own* (first published in 1929) is a plea for a specifically female space in the intellectual world, but *Three Guineas* (published in 1938) is a more determined attack on the conventional articulation of masculinity.

What Woolf saw in the modern world (and by the time of writing *Three Guineas* she had been able to observe both the potential for military destruction in the First World War and the rise of Fascism in the 1930s) was a fusion of the apparently 'natural' elements of masculinity with a rigid and hierarchical elaboration of appropriately male behaviour. She established links between masculinity and the institutional world of modernity: no one looking at the photographs contained in *Three Guineas* could fail to see Woolf's argument that modern institutional life is made and preserved for men. But what Woolf does not do – and in this she differs from both her own feminist contemporaries and those of later generations – is argue that institutional power is in some sense 'naturally' male, while women inhabit a different, kinder and less power-obsessed space. Woolf does not want women to seek power – not for her the attack on the 'glass ceilings' named by elements of contemporary feminism as appropriate goals for achievement by women. On the contrary, what Woolf suggests is a deconstruction of the nature of power itself, so that institutions are organized rather more in terms of specific aims and rather less in terms of the self-serving ambitions of their personnel. There is a passage in *Three Guineas* which is worth quoting in full, because it contains Woolf's fierce hatred of the rigid politics of gender, and also because, in its emphasis on the idea of 'the infantile fixation in the fathers', it articulates Woolf's belief in the location of the inhibition of women's intellectual and imaginative creativity: the acquiesence with, and acceptance of, 'male' paternal authority:

> But the fathers were met, as the nineteenth century drew on, by a force which had become so strong in its turn that it is much to be hoped that the psychologists will find some name for it. The old names as we have seen are futile and false, 'Feminism', we have had to destroy. 'The emancipation of women' is equally inexpressive and corrupt. To say that the daughters were inspired prematurely by the principles of anti-Fascism is merely to repeat the fashionable and hideous jargon of the moment. To

call them champions of intellectual liberty and culture is to cloud
the air with the dust of lecture halls and the damp dowdiness of
public meetings.[6]

Virginia Woolf is accepted as a central figure in the history of the fiction
of modernity, but rather less so as a figure in the social history and social
theory of modernity. Yet her claims to this second status are legitimate, in
that she made connections between the personal and institutional (as had
Simmel and Weber), and also showed us how – literally – our gender was at
least in part the product of our imagination. (As Woolf wrote, 'It suggests
that the public and the private worlds are inseparably connected; that the
tyrannies and servilities of the one are the tyrannies and servilities of the
other'.)[7] Woolf – and the Bloomsbury Group as a whole – were pilloried and
loathed by many of their contemporaries for what was seen as their distance
from the 'real' world, yet two outstanding figures in the Group – Virginia
Woolf herself and John Maynard Keynes – were both much concerned
with the material and what can be described as the 'real' world. *A Room of
One's Own* is explicitly about money and Keynes' attack on the Treaty of
Versailles in *The Economic Consequences of the Peace* is a passionate plea
for the recognition of the implications of decisions about material resources.[8]
In both cases what is interesting in the work of these figures is their recogni-
tion of the 'strictly material' within their capacity for the imaginative.

If we return to Jervis' remark about the kind of person necessary for
modernity we find his phrase 'the self-disciplined structure of personhood'.
That description at first might suggest a certain kind of capacity rather than
a set of particular ideas and values. But if we start to consider the meaning
of the phrase, and indeed other phrases similar to it made by others such as
Weber, we are confronted by an implicit set of values about the nature
of the 'appropriate person' for modernity. As was suggested in Chapter 3,
Weber defined the attributes of the person imbued with the Protestant ethic
– a person whose life and work were dedicated to serving a particular set of
values and a particular relationship between God and the material world.
Jervis' comment (about self-discipline) is less explicitly contextual and thus
the person whom he constructs as the ideal citizen of modernity is less
closely related (if related at all) to capitalism and capitalist social relations.
The self-disciplined person is capable of relating to (and emerging from)
any bureaucratic structure, be it a multinational corporation, a state socialist ministry or a society of classical antiquity. In this analysis, bureaucracy
itself is the seed-ground for the personality: for Weber (and for Simmel and
most obviously for Marx) the seed-ground is not just a bureaucracy *per se*,
but a specific *form* of bureaucracy which has a relationship to a specific
form of material relations.

The wish to maintain a sense of alternative priorities and agendas in late
modernity (or late capitalism) is sometimes extraordinarily difficult in the

face of social evidence which suggests that any bureaucracy, whatever its stated purpose, needs a certain kind of person as an employee. Thus distinctions between working for a public or private corporation or institution disappear in contemporary forms of organization and cultures which validate and encourage 'managerialism'. Within this social world there is considerable reason to assume that 'working for Ford' may be just the same as working for Oxfam. This is as much part of depoliticization as low turnouts throughout the West in elections: the demonstration of the impact on individual actions, and sense of agency, of a 'McDonaldized' culture which has effectively minimized political difference, not through repression or terror but through the acceptance of the legitimacy of bureaucratic order.[9] Within this social space, there can be little sense of radically divisive social issues: late capitalism, it can appear, ensures an acceptable level of existence for two thirds of the population in every western society and is disinclined to engage in military conflict within its boundaries.

This account of late capitalism – familiar to readers of writers as diverse as Marcuse, Habermas and Fukuyama – suggests that contemporary social theory has to come to terms with societies in which conflict is no longer structural (in the terms of Marx) but aspirational.[10] That is to say, social conflict is today what E.J. Hobsbawm has described as 'life style politics': disagreements (albeit fundamental and of crucial importance to individuals) about sexual orientation or way of life.[11] In this model of the social world, individuals have apparently accepted, post-1989, that capitalism is the 'only game in town' and that the erosion of trade union membership and influence, as well as the disappearance of the rhetoric of structural political difference, is inevitable. 'Real' politics, writers about the West have suggested, are now about sexual choice and the environment rather than about social class and economic inequality. As long ago as 1970 the Romanian-born sociologist Lucien Goldmann commented that in the twentieth (and presumably also the twenty-first) century the real political struggle would be not for control of the means of production but for control of consciousness: the crucial struggle in the twenty-first century is for access to the control of culture, rather than production.[12] Similarly, although more recently, Nigel Thrift has emphasized the global prevalence of 'managerialist discourse' in which exploitation (of both managers and workers) is obscured.[13]

In Britain this argument was put most fully in the 1980s by Stuart Hall. Hall argued that politics had become 'cultural politics' and that political debates were increasingly about individual choices and decisions.[14] In part, this view was derived from the political experience of the 1980s when right-wing governments in both Britain and the USA (the years of Thatcher and Reagan) seemed to be effective in ensuring that the ideological battle between the left and right was very firmly won by the right. The 'market' (and capitalism) were coupled together in such a way as to ensure that it became taken for granted that only capitalism (which often was known by the less abrasive term 'market economy') could ensure democracy and personal freedom. The old Soviet Union had been no advertisement for the sense of personal freedom and choice as constructed in the West, and its demise was hailed as a sign of the coming to maturity and democracy of the world's second greatest superpower. Within this seismic shift in world politics, and the rapid disappearance of those East–West rivalries which had been the political reality of the world since the end of the Second World War, social theory has had to reposition itself and rethink – as Hall's work demonstrates – its relationship to a new political reality. In a time when countries that were once almost hermetically sealed satellite states of Moscow petition to join the European Union, there lies an intellectual challenge to theories about the social world.

Perhaps the most important aspect of this challenge, and one which relates directly to questions of gender, is that which concerns the meaning, origins and determination of the idea of 'culture'. For social theory in the first half of the twentieth century, culture had two specific meanings. First, the sense of culture as also understood by anthropology, meaning the values and expectations of people in a particular society. This understanding assumed if not a shared normative framework in every society, then at least some recognition of the 'dominant' or the 'common' culture as it was then called. It was assumed that shared cultural values could be identified in every society, even if individual sociologists differed in their understanding and explanation of the origins of 'culture'. For Marxists, culture was related (in varying degrees of simplicity) to the material basis of society. The famous statement by Marx that in 'every epoch the ruling ideas are the ideas of the ruling class' was accepted as the starting point for an examination of culture. Second, culture was understood in terms of its products – less the lived experience than the actual artefacts of the culture.

In both senses, the general thesis of western social theory until the latter part of the twentieth century was that 'culture' could be understood in terms of a model of dominance and dissent. From the 1930s onwards critics of the mass culture of the West – from the Frankfurt School to Christopher Caudwell and Georg Lukacs – had all endorsed the view that 'culture' could be seen in terms of systems of experience and products of culture which were related, albeit with different degrees of complexity, to the *class* structure of the West.[15] Indeed, until the end of the 1950s, actual empirical observation by historians and social scientists suggested, as Richard Hoggart had argued, that culture and class were very closely related and that the boundaries between classes were maintained and policed through cultural difference.[16]

But in the 1960s the culture of the West began to change, and with it the understanding of that culture also shifted. There had been important work in the 1950s (notably, in Britain, by Raymond Williams and Richard

Hoggart) to demonstrate the existence of working-class cultures as vital and as coherent as those of the middle class, but these exercises in reclamation (which were to continue in the 1970s and 80s through the notable work in Britain of History Workshop and in particular Ralph Samuel) continued to assume cultural stratification and difference in terms of class.[17] In the 1960s two changes occurred: first, western culture itself changed, to become both increasingly global and increasingly age segmented; and second, the theoretical understanding of culture, fuelled by the work of Foucault and Lyotard, itself began to change, and change dramatically. Poststructuralism, deconstruction and psychoanalysis became part of the theoretical language of the study of literature, and subsequently became equally significant to sociology. Indeed, sociology – which in the 1960s had appeared as an intellectually radical discipline – came to seem redundant as cultural studies assumed a more commanding space in the theoretical universe. Sociology's emphasis on social class – which can now be read as radical and innovative – came to be seen as lacking, in that this analysis ignored both racial and gender difference and refused what was identified as a degree of classlessness of late twentieth-century culture. Within the terms of this analysis, Mrs Thatcher's (and John Major's) determination to produce a 'classless' Britain was a direct expression of the *Zeitgeist*: an apparently classless politics for an apparently classless society. Those who pointed out that poverty was still a significant factor on both sides of the Atlantic were condemned for refusing to acknowledge that it was as much a matter of 'cultural' (and cultural deprivation and exclusion) as structural inequality.

The problem with attacks on this view is that the relationship between culture and poverty, and culture and other forms of inequality, is complex. For example, feminist sociologists have demonstrated for generations (from the work of Mirra Komarovsky in the late 1940s) that women – and particularly adolescent girls – are fearful of achievement because of fears about its detrimental effect on heterosexual attractiveness.[18] Although this belief, and the behaviour associated with it, may have largely disappeared in many sections of the western middle class, what is important about the thesis that Komarovsky advanced is that culture can, if not determine, at least define the way in which individuals behave in the social world, and that that behaviour does not immediately relate to the economic and the material. A counter-argument to Komarovsky's proposition is that she actually demonstrated very clearly the relationship of women to the material world: in a society in which women have little or no access to well-paid employment, and where there are specific barriers to the employment of women, it is economically rational for women to maximize the possibilities of their material well-being by marriage to well-paid men. Both middle-class and working-class women had been encouraged to enter paid employment during the Second World War, but once this ended the barriers to women's employment (e.g. the marriage rules in the British civil service and teaching profession) returned.

The cultural changes of the 1960s dissolved those norms which, in the 1950s, had made divorce in the West an aberrant experience. Marriage was no longer the secure relationship which it was once believed to be: for women the sexual liberation of the 1960s brought freedom to be sexually and professionally autonomous, but it also brought an end to the idea that it was more economically rational to compete *for* men rather than *against* them. This cultural change has now made an impact upon state policies towards education and employment since it is now an expectation that schools will encourage the achievements of girls as much as boys and that employers will not discriminate on the grounds of gender. We recognize the existence of these changes in our daily lives, since they are clear both in terms of specific institutional arrangements and in terms of the different experiences of women of different generations. But accounting for them, and suggesting social explanations for them, is a different matter. An exclusively economic explanation would explain the social changes of the 1960s in terms of the needs of a capitalist system geared to individual consumption: this is a form of society which has to ensure the effective participation as a consumer of every member of society. Thus, for example, a married woman who remains at home to care for children may be ineffective as a consumer. Equally, the standard of living to which she, and her family, aspire may be impossible to achieve with only one household income. Since changing codes about sexual behaviour have made it more likely that marriage will end in divorce, it is also important that women have some access to income other than that of the possibly unreliable support of the departed spouse.

But in setting out this vignette of family life in the West in the twenty-first century (in which divorce is dramatically more commonplace than in the first 60 years of the twentieth century) it is immediately apparent that we confront a mix of economic and cultural realities. The changed economic reality of the West is that many sections of the population cannot survive, as households, on the income of the male partner. But the changed culture of the West is one in which our expectations about 'survival' have changed between generations. Consumer credit has made possible levels of consumer spending which were unknown 40 years ago: home ownership is one example of the way in which credit is now actively offered rather than grudgingly allowed. Women and men becoming adults in the West in the last 30 years of the twentieth century became adults in a world of sexual permissiveness, available consumer credit and a labour market which is increasingly, although far from totally, losing its gendered character. For sociology, this 'new world' was characterized by the apparent relative absence of cultural class differentiation. What then, could (and can) sociology explain which cultural studies cannot?

One answer to this question, which has led to an important debate within feminism, is that the technological innovation of the late twentieth century has created an entirely novel set of social relationships in which traditional distinctions, not just of gender or race, but also of nation, have become insignificant. Scott Lash is among those who have proposed that the social world of the late twentieth and twenty-first centuries – with its emphasis on what Lash describes as a 'de-differentiation' – is fundamentally and qualitatively different from that of the early and middle twentieth century.[19] Definitions of boundaries and communities have changed, as has the impact on individuals of individual difference. Judith Butler, as we have seen, has argued for the 'politics of recognition' as the appropriate politics of the twenty-first century – essentially a form of politics which is directed towards the achievement of the equal legitimacy of all sexual and personal choices. Nancy Fraser has suggested that this is, in point of fact, exactly what global capitalism would wish to achieve: the continuation of prejudices and discriminations about sexuality or race are counterproductive to the global capitalist enterprise. Without stating it explicitly, Nancy Fraser's argument suggests that a politics of recognition is actually in the best interests of capitalism: the cultural redundancy of homophobia or misogyny is absolute in an era in which effective participation in consumption is of crucial importance. Fraser suggests that it is only through continuing to ague for redistribution that we can begin to move towards real human equality: as long as recognition is not accompanied by redistribution then gender (and racial) difference will continue to be amplified by class inequality.

It must be apparent to any citizen of any western society in the twenty-first century that there are increasingly very few forms of employment which are *in themselves* gender specific. Nevertheless, the connection between gender and skill (which Anne Phillips and Barbara Taylor defined in 1980) remains, and impacts upon the differential incomes of women and men in full-time employment.[20] What also remains is the close association between men and institutional power: the class structure of western societies is such that while few men have access to significant institutional power the numbers are still more limited for women. Concepts such as the 'glass ceiling' are used to explain the absence of women from institutional power and a considerable literature demonstrates that the characteristics most often associated with institutional success are those most often associated with men and male socialization. Personal qualities such as aggression and risk-taking – located and legitimated more often in men than in women – underpin success, or are assumed to underpin success, in any number of contexts.

In this context we meet, again, that complex mix of arguments about nature and nurture which inform (or confuse) discussion about the relationship between gender and social behaviour. For example, we know, as social fact, that men dominate the significant institutions of all western societies. But we are still undecided about the reasons for this, in part because of contemporary (and indeed long-lasting) scepticism about the value of institutional achievement for either sex, and in part because of a cultural suspicion about those women who aspire to unconventional levels of achievement. For example, George Eliot wrote, in the second half of the nineteenth century, that the further emancipation of women (by which she meant further entry by women into public life) would alter women beyond 'tolerable' expectations.[21] This, we must remember, was before England's Married Women's Property Act of 1882, the enfranchisement of women or any significant attempt to educate women. In the twenty-first century we accept aspects of gender equality that would have horrified George Eliot, yet at the same time it is important to recognize those patterns of compensatory femininity which are still expected (and colluded with) by women who become publicly successful. Mrs Thatcher's self-identification with the housewifely skills which she clearly seldom practised was a testament to the 'cultural lag' about women and power. Throughout the West there are no formal boundaries to prevent women achieving the same range of social goals as men, but the cultural inhibitions remain. These cultural inhibitions are closely related to naturalistic expectations about gender-specific behaviour: men should be aggressive, women should not.

There is an extensive literature, both fictional and otherwise, which demonstrates the misery inflicted upon human beings by rigidly enforced gender stereotypes: women who have spent their lives in domestic drudgery and men who have endured jobs that they have loathed in the name of social expectations. We might now assume at the beginning of the twenty-first century that nobody 'has to' accept a particular gender stereotype, but that optimism ignores the social evidence which suggests that gender stereotyping, although less rigid (and essentially less dichotomized between 'male' and 'female') nevertheless still affects all of us in personally, as well as in socially, significant ways. Same-sex relationships are now publicly possible, as is the public discussion of sexuality and sexual expectations. But studies of adolescents suggest that peer pressures are as rigid about gender appropriate behaviour as they ever were, and that the ancient confusions of adolescence remain articulated within a limited set of social and sexual boundaries. Thus socialization remains a process in which ideals of masculinity and femininity are constructed, and constructed in ways which can still create the same pressures, miseries and uncertainties as they ever did.[22]

In assessing the evidence about gender socialization we need, therefore, as much information from history and literature as we do from sociology. Indeed, there are important grounds for arguing that the 'merely' sociological ignores the way in which social life is constantly in a process of both change and immobility. The snapshot impressions produced by sociological studies inform us of the reality of the moment, but it is only through a sense of history, comparative analysis and longitudinal method that we can begin to distinguish socially significant change from the purely ephemeral. Fashion, one of the mass experiences of the twentieth century, often deludes individuals into assuming the world is changing: women in short skirts, men with long hair, both sexes with tattoos and body piercing are known to cause consternation among members of different generations. Yet these examples of the ways in which people adorn and display their bodies are only part of an ongoing process of body alteration: what we often do not see when we look at people dressed or behaving in apparently unconventional ways is the continuity in patterns of behaviour across generations. Examples within English culture of continuity in behaviour are many and varied: for example, the hippies of the 1960s were part of an ancient Bohemian tradition within English culture. Bohemia, as Elizabeth Wilson has pointed out, has been part of English life since the end of the eighteenth century.[23] Equally, the environmentalists often associated in the public mind with the late twentieth century have close social and intellectual links with earlier concerns – for example those expressed by Rachel Carson in 1962 in *Silent Spring* – about factory farming and the destruction of the natural environment.[24]

Precisely because we can identify continuities within our culture, so it is all the more important to emphasize this within a sociological context, since otherwise sociology becomes in a very real sense a 'fashion victim'. That is, sociology, in refusing the knowledge of history and literature, assumes that what is novel is also new or innovative. The form may very well be 'new' but often the underlying cause or relationship is long-standing. Sociological memory, and the development of this phenomenon, is as important in the context of gender as any other, and its importance has three aspects. First, we must note that both sexes have protested, for centuries, about stereotypical expectations. Women, as long as history has been written, have demanded (as Marlene Le Gates has pointed out) the same social rights as their brothers or husbands.[25] Men have long wished to escape from those forms of behaviour (specifically physical prowess) which are expected of 'real' men. Second, western societies (and Britain and the USA are no exception) have been contradictory about their gendered expectations: women have been assumed to be frail and timid at the same time as they have been expected to raise large families or work long hours in factories. Finally, men are thought to be capable of defining the heights of cultural and artistic achievement while maintaining personal self-discipline and emotional continence. Strength is expected of women at the same time as sensitivity is acknowledged in men: a reversal of many of the stereotypes which are sometimes assumed to be dominant.

As much as we should acknowledge the paradoxes of many of our ideas about gender, so we should also remember two other aspects of what has been described above as 'sociological memory'. These are, first, the considerable impact which deliberate strategies and policies about gender (whether of the state or commerce) can have on the behaviour of men and women. On many occasions this impact is merely ephemeral: fashion can persuade some members of both sexes to disport themselves in particular styles. But on other occasions the needs of the state can be such as to produce a determined attempt to change or modify conventional patterns of gendered behaviour. The most telling example here is the policy towards women and paid work by governments in Britain and the USA during the Second World War. Faced with a shortage of male labour, both governments deliberately created female heroines who worked in factories and as support staff in the armed services. 'Rosie the Riveter' may not have personified the actual experience of women in the Second World War, but she personified a new (and deliberately created) ideology about women. The second point that needs to be made here about sociological memory is that it often fails to acknowledge that individual lives are a complex mixture of the past, the present and the future, with aspirations located in each of these historical periods. Thus we may recall our childhood and adolescence, and long to return to them or leave them well behind, but as much as we have different attitudes to the past, so we have to the present and the future. Indeed, our perceptions of the past are often a crucial ingredient of our understanding of the present, in that we wish to recreate in the present what we feel we have lost.

These remarks about memory and collective attitudes to the past are an important part of the way in which we construct our ideas about gender. In the past 40 years it is notable that the West has seen the emergence of a literature about childhood and adolescence which stresses the uncertainties which many people have faced in identifying and confronting their sexuality, and autobiographical literature has stressed the discomfort children experienced in their own lives in part because of the recognition of the unhappiness of their parents.[26] What these accounts emphasize is the misery experienced by parents who were forced to live out lives in patterns which accorded with conventional expectations about 'a wife' or 'a mother' or 'a husband'. Writing in her autobiographical account of childhood, Lorna Sage comments:

> Here we have the family of the period: self-made and going places. Only when you look more closely can you see that this housewife is pathologically scared of food, hates home, is really a child dreaming of pretty things and treats; and that this businessman will never accumulate capital, he's still a boy soldier, going over the top again and again. Their obsessions had met, fallen in love and married; they completed and sustained each other.[27]

The word that needs emphasis here is that of obsessions, since it is in that word that we can find the most direct reference to the socially created.

Fantasy, and fantasies about others, are an ancient part of civilization, but what we need to identify in any sociological understanding is the part that socially created fantasies play in our imagination both about ourselves and about others. The fantasies pursued by Lorna Sage's parents were – at least according to their daughter – fantasies about business success and marriage as the gateway to a golden life. The evident incapacities of the two parents doomed these fantasies to failure – but the ideas, and ideals, about how life should be remained.

A great deal of recent autobiographical literature by relatively successful children about their pasts is concerned with the decade of the 1950s, a decade in which the West recreated the nuclear family in terms appropriate to the emergence of a consumer society. In this family and this home, children were raised and regulated within a suburban dream, a dream sustained by economic plenty and undisturbed by problems about sex, drugs or rock n' roll.[28] For millions of people in Britain and the USA (and most particularly black people in the USA) this dream had no basis in fact or lived experience. But it was nevertheless an influential dream in which cohesive nuclear families were sustained by male labour in the workplace and female labour in the home. It was a model of the social world inappropriately exported to countries outside the West, and it was (and is) a model of the social world endlessly (and pointlessly) defended by politicians on both sides of the Atlantic.[29] The 'antisocial family', as Michele Barrett and Mary McIntosh have described it, was extensively criticized in the 1960s and 70s: Aaron Esterson, R.D. Laing and David Cooper were among those men who attacked what they saw as a damaging and punitive mythology about the family.[30] Fiction and non-fiction joined in a chorus of complaint about the western nuclear family, a chorus in which Philip Larkin's assertion that 'They fuck you up, your mum and dad' became the most often quoted summary.[31]

Larkin may have written that parents were responsible for the miseries of their children, but as sociologists we have a responsibility to remember that society also 'fucks up' (to borrow Larkin's verb) individuals. The example of the history of the family in the second half of the twentieth century provides an excellent example of the intersection of the personal and social, and an example which should encourage us to consider carefully the extent to which 'mum and dad' are really and truly the source of individual misery. As noted above, the family which was made the ideal of the West in the years after the Second World War was one in which it was taken for granted that women's work lay in the home. For example, in 1944 the Beveridge Report, which established the provision of social security in Britain, explicitly excluded married women from inclusion in its list of insured people.[32] Married women, the thinking went, were provided for by their husbands. Within this pattern, unmarried women with children did not exist, and neither did the 'dual earner' households which have now become commonplace throughout the West. The social world was divided into the home and the public space, and it was thought appropriate to exclude women, particulary married women, from that public space. Indeed, until 1949, married women had to resign if employed in the administrative civil service in Britain and many state schools refused to employ them.

We now know that this world was never as completely homogeneous as was once supposed, as we also know that there was protest about these social arrangements. But in terms of sociological theory we can also remark that theoretically this world was largely taken for granted. The nuclear family, the exclusion of women from the workforce and the assumption of the normality of the pattern of female economic dependence were assumed to be 'normal'. On neither side of the Atlantic did sociologists question the order of this world, and while a few women (e.g. Viola Klein) questioned expectations about gender relations, their work was often regarded as marginal.[33] Yet that work had one feature which remains consistently important: the ideas that the 'female character' (as Viola Klein was to describe it in 1946) is not born, but made. Once this comment had been voiced (if not for the first time, then at least most emphatically in the twentieth century) it became possible to begin to denaturalize the male and the female.

This process of denaturalization – of regarding with scepticism the idea that men and women naturally fulfil certain social roles – was extensively proposed in the 1960s and 70s. The first attacks came from feminists, who argued that sociology was guilty of complicity in patriarchal expectations by refusing to problematize social roles and social expectations related to gender. A second form of attack came from gay and lesbian theorists who argued that not only did sociology refuse the complexities of gender, but it refused those complexities from a position of unthinking heterosexuality. 'Compulsory heterosexuality' as Adrienne Rich described the sexual code of the West in 1980, was taken to task for its rejection of homosexuality and its homophobic assumptions about sexual identity.[34] The influence of Michel Foucault was pivotal in determining arguments which accounted for sexual identity in terms of constructed 'discourses' rather than naturalistic givens.[35] Ken Plummer and Mary McIntosh were among those sociologists in Britain who argued that sexual identity was created, while the historian Jeffrey Weeks showed how sexual identity had changed across time and culture.[36] By the end of the 1970s it would have been a foolhardy or professionally suicidal sociologist who would have been prepared to argue that sexual identity was anything other than constructed. Socialization into gender and socialization about sex were seen as part of a process in which society created particular kinds of boys and girls, women and men and sexual behaviour.[37]

But just as society, and theories of social construction, seemed to have taken the upper hand in debates about the acquisition of gendered identity, two important interventions were made. Neither of these took for granted social response to gender difference (in many ways both interventions were highly critical of it) but they did allow that significant, inevitable differences existed between men and women. These interventions were those of Juliet Mitchell and Carol Gilligan. Juliet Mitchell's *Psychoanalysis and Feminism* was published in 1974, and Carol Gilligan's *In a Different Voice* in 1982.[38] Although their work is theoretically distinct in other ways, both women emphasized the difference which the fact of biological sexual identity made to social behaviour. In neither case, it must be emphatically said, did the author assume that the social response to gender differences was to be accepted or deemed appropriate. Mitchell and Gilligan both wanted to change the social response to gender (and in this they have remained consistent). Both, however, wanted the social world to recognize difference – to accept that norms and normality have been constructed as male, but need not necessarily remain so. Juliet Mitchell's *Psychoanalysis and Feminism* was to establish a basis through which a generation of both sociologists and literary critics radically reread and reinterpreted the classic literature of the West (largely, though not exclusively, its classic fiction) to demonstrate the instability, rather than the supposed stability, of gender identities. Jacqueline Rose and Terry Castle are among the many feminist literary critics who have demonstrated that the resolution of gendered identity was never assured and was always problematic.[39]

While these arguments were being made in the context of literary criticism, feminist interpretations of psychoanalysis were being equally disturbing within politics and sociology. The relationship of Carol Gilligan's work to psychoanalysis was always more distant than that of Juliet Mitchell, but Gilligan, although less concerned with the practice and the theory of psychoanalysis, took issue with one of the key concepts of post-Freudian literature: the idea that the super-ego of women is less developed than that of men. As Gilligan pointed out, this view (most coherently expressed by Kohlberg) made women into moral infants. Unlike men, Kohlberg argued, women would not 'do' morality, in that they were unable to distinguish between the subjective and the objective. In her study of a group of women faced with the possibility of abortion, Gilligan demonstrated that women did not think of moral questions in terms of abstract questions about right and wrong, but in terms of the possible impact (for good or bad) of decisions on others. This form of moral discourse, in which intentions and outcomes are as important as the theoretical viability of the argument, is not inferior or superior to 'male' moral reasoning, but different. It is on this issue of difference that Gilligan's work has been so influential, since the implication of her thesis is that the moral discourse of the West, and the institutions constructed around it, has been 'male' in the form of its construction. For political scientists, as much as sociologists, this argument is (and should be) immensely disturbing, since it brings into question the terms in which we judge and assess all social questions. Gilligan's work has not been without its detractors (particularly on the question of its implicit essentialism) but it has put moral issues and moral questions very firmly on the social agenda, since she asks us to consider the question of whose interests social rule and social expectations have been designed to serve.[40] Many sociologists have always assumed that this is an easy question to answer, and follow Marx's thesis that 'in every epoch the ruling ideas are the ideas of the ruling class'. However, after Gilligan that idea is far less sustainable, since she forces us to confront the reality of ruling ideas being not just the preserve of a ruling class, but a particular gender (that of men) within the ruling class. Gilligan brings us very rapidly to the question of whether or not it is accurate to argue, from the most everyday and most domestic to the most institutional and rational, that it is a man's world. If this is the case, then what social theory has to confront is the fact of 'ruling ideas' that are not just class-, but gender-specific.

Thirty or 40 years ago many social theorists (feminists and otherwise) might have been prepared to argue that men did control the institutional and ideological structures of late capitalism. In institutional terms, men were predominant in positions of power and authority and in ideological terms men were the authors of the most significant social narratives of the law, representation and the moral order. 'The male gaze' as generations of critics after John Berger were to describe it, was essentially the lens through which women were seen in culture.[41] As feminists pointed out, considerable industries existed which were exclusively about the portrayal of women for men's view. Catherine MacKinnon, Andrea Dworkin and Sheila Jeffreys – from different theoretical positions and in different cultural contexts – contributed widely influential arguments which suggested that women (and women's bodies) were a commodity at the disposal of male interests.[42] What these arguments did was to position 'men' and 'the male' against 'women' and the 'female' and to offer a view of the social world which was structured by gender. The thesis was less widely influential in its entirety than in its influence in specific cases and instances: for example, Sue Lees' work on rape (and the trials of rape victims) owed much, implicitly, to Catherine MacKinnon and her arguments about gender inequalities in the processes and assumptions of law.[43]

Thus in a number of institutional contexts (and the law on both sides of the Atlantic was a much cited example) it was possible to demonstrate that interests identified with men rather than women prevailed. In terms of social action, where that leaves women is in a position of defence and reaction. Indeed, a review of the history of feminism in the West demonstrates plainly that women have consistently fought for social rights and privileges that men have already achieved. Moreover, in order to do this women have generally had to adopt those forms of behaviour and aspiration which are synonymous with participation and success in particular contexts. The well known adage that in order to succeed women have to be twice as clever as men suggests public recognition of a pattern of compensation with which women have to accord in order to succeed. Even though feminist postcards may suggest that being twice as competent as a man is hardly difficult, it remains demonstrably clear that gender discrimination still exists throughout western institutions.

Gilligan's work does not attempt to challenge the evidence which suggests that men occupy controlling positions in institutional and ideological structures. But what she does do is to introduce the view into social theory that women's voices are seldom heard in the social world and that those voices become muted at adolescence. The 'absence of female desire', as Michelle Fine has described it, is an absence of sexual desire, but we might also suggest that what is largely absent from the social world is that female moral understanding which Gilligan argued had a distinct pattern.[44] Here recent debates about the 'feminization' of western culture become significant. The thesis is broadly that western culture is acquiring new subjectivities and identities and that within the culture as a whole there is more acceptance and anticipation of emotional need and emotional life.[45] 'Emotional literacy' has become a much vaunted, and credible, part of human behaviour. We are expected to be 'emotionally literate' and thus capable of recognizing the impact of our own emotional behaviour (and that of others) on our choices and our actions. Hence British social commentators were much exercised by the public reaction to the death of Princess Diana. The extraordinary scenes of public grief (and the equally public assumption by other members of the Royal Family that such grief was inappropriate) suggested that the culture had changed, and that the expression of loss and grief was publicly acceptable, and indeed laudable.

To this thesis other critics replied that public grief at the death of notable public figures was not unknown.[46] Despite the scale of the public mourning, it was suggested that no general thesis about changes in male and female behaviour could be built on the events of one week. In terms of social theory, however, there is an explanation which is more convincing than most about these events: namely Weber's argument that as we become more 'rational' in our behaviour, so we seek ways of expressing those feelings which are ever more consistently repressed in our daily lives. Our 'ordered lives' seek outlets for expression and in this pattern neither men nor women have exclusive access to the emotional and the apparently irrational. Acts of public rage ('road rage', 'traffic rage' and the other rages of urban life) become the inevitable consequence of an over-ordered universe, rather than the expression of a new emotional reality.

Acts of public rage such as attacks on other road users receive media attention and comment and are generally interpreted as the result of frustrations arising from the complexities of contemporary urban life. Other forms of rage, however, are more general and suggest that in periods of stress we often attack ourselves rather than others. Two aspects of self-attack are suicide and eating disorders: two conditions which appear to follow gender patterns, in that men commit suicide more often than women, while women are more often subject to eating disorders. Explanations of both these forms of self-attack invoke ideas about gender. For example, the greater suicide rate among men is explained in terms of men's greater social isolation coupled with their greater competence in acts of aggression, including those directed against themselves.[47] In explaining the prevalence of eating disorders among women, Susan Bordo had suggested three 'axes' as she calls them, which disempower women and lead them to attack their bodies.[48] These are: Cartesian dualism, the western celebration of will-power and emotional control and the gender/power relationship of the West. Essentially, women learn to fear their bodies, and fears that cannot be controlled have in some way to be punished.

In these explanations (and indeed in others associated with discussions of the body) it is not assumed that the West is becoming more emotionally literate and understanding. Indeed, the theses of Bordo *et al.* suggest the exact opposite: that we are becoming less able to develop those emotional selves which will enable us to live effectively. The culture may have progressed considerably in theoretical terms in that we have become more competent in the theoretical understanding of aspects of emotional life, but for many individuals the world in which they live offers not emotional support but emotional insecurity and concern. Hence, it may be possible to identify specific instances in which western culture offers more social space and more social legitimacy for expressions of 'the feminine' but the culture as a whole is one in which gender remains a potent social divide. Hence no explanation of suicide rates has superseded that of Durkheim, who observed in 1897 the greater social integration of women and the emotional protection which that offered.[49] Nor have theories about women and eating disorders fundamentally developed the understanding which male authors of the eighteenth and nineteenth centuries had of the relationship of women to their bodies – namely that in periods of stress and emotional loss, women punish their bodies and themselves rather than the sources of their misery. When Clarissa Harlowe starved herself to death in Samuel Richardson's eighteenth-century novel, she became the first woman in western fiction to demonstrate the capacity which women have (just as much as men) to kill themselves when life becomes intolerable. If we see eating disorders as a form of suicide, then what emerges is an equalization of the possibilities of human misery for women and men, rather than similar means of self-destruction. It is impossible to distinguish between the miseries of the male suicide and the female anorexic, except in the form that the misery takes. It is thus important in reviewing information and theoretical accounts about women and men in relation to their bodies to recognize that human unhappiness knows no distinctions of gender, but *expressions* of unhappiness do.

It is one of the many instances in social life in which gender both matters and makes no difference – a complexity, a contradiction and a paradox which makes gender such an inherently unstable part of social theory. That relationship is as turbulent and as contested as that of any marriage or long-term relationship.

CHAPTER 6

NOW YOU SEE IT, NOW YOU DON'T

In the past 50 years there have been a number of warnings about what Alvin Gouldner once described as the 'coming crisis of western sociology'.[1] In terms that are similar to those of the far left, sociologists have been fond of announcing the 'crisis' and the demise, if not of industrial capitalism, then at least of sociological theory. Gouldner's crisis was, of course, somewhat deflected by the emergence of postmodernism: in an essentially plural theoretical universe, a universe without powerful organizing narratives, the possibility of crisis is diminished. There can be a crisis of absence, but a crisis brought about by the loss of authority and legitimacy of a particular organizing discourse is lessened in a theoretical world in which no single explanation or theory has a monopoly of credibility. However, before postmodernism became the lingua franca of academic debate, C. Wright Mills had warned sociologists in the 1950s that if they did not attempt to 'construct a structural whole' then they would lose sight of what he saw as sociology's engagement with a critical account of society.[2]

That assumption, that sociology *has* a critical engagement with the social world, made Mills somewhat atypical in the academic world. Like his later equally eminent compatriot Noam Chomsky, Mills made no secret of his view that the USA was a military-industrial state which was organized around and towards the maintenance of a particular kind of political and social order – that of political individualism and a capitalist political economy. Mills (and to a certain extent Chomsky) wrote before the end of the cold war, the coming of the market to the Soviet Union and the global political domination of capitalism as the 'only game in town'. In that political era, it was perhaps significantly easier to be a critic of the West and its social theory because there existed (if even in a flawed form) the possibility of an alternative to the market economy. Sociology and sociological theory could be informed by a sense of political difference and dichotomy which was to disappear in the 1970s and 80s. Although the revolution in Russia in 1917 was consistently regarded by historians (as well as sociologists) with scepticism, there nevertheless remained a sense that socialism and socialist politics could be directed towards the establishment of both an equitable and a democratic society.

After the fall of the Berlin Wall in 1989 state socialism, together with the Marxist-Leninist political ideology which had underpinned it, was consigned to the historical graveyard. A new generation of historians, such as Orlando Figes, who were writing outside previous boundaries of 'left' and 'right', saw the Soviet Union as a country constructed through terror, anti-democratic and in some ways significantly worse than the state which it replaced.[3] The 'death of history' was accompanied in much of the West by a decline in political interest, demonstrated by the failure of significant numbers of western populations to vote in their local or national elections, except (as in Australia) when actually forced to do so. De-politicization became a noted characteristic of the West, a loss of interest in national politics which was accompanied by theoretical accounts of contemporary politics (for example by Bob Jessop) which suggested the emergence of the 'internationalized state'.[4] Elsewhere in this book I have argued that sociological analysis can have the status of a photograph: it can provide accurate descriptions of a society, or an aspect of a society, but without a sense of narrative the description has the ontological status of a snapshot. It is that sense of narrative which a number of sociologists – for example, Giddens and Mouzelis – have attempted to reclaim.[5] Neither has claimed the politics of C. Wright Mills (although Mouzelis is probably closer to Mills than Giddens) but what distinguishes their work is a sense, albeit muted, that the best sociology emerges from moral commitment and political engagement and not from the assumption of the 'neutral' observer.

In attempting to maintain a sense of sociology's place in this epistemological world, Giddens and Mouzelis have moved close to the political space occupied by feminist sociologists and feminist historians of ideas. The entry of second-wave feminism into the academy in the 1970s was motivated by politics – and a politics of both the public and the private worlds. Harold Wilson once famously denounced a 'group of politically motivated men' who had the temerity – of all things – to challenge a political judgement. But the remark was, and is, evocative of the late twentieth and early twenty-first centuries' sense that somehow 'politics' are no longer necessary, and only cause divisions and disruption. The feminist academics of the 1970s had a strong sense of politics – and that sense was indicative in the rewriting and rethinking of disciplines across the social sciences and the humanities. What feminism did in the academy (and in sociology as much as in other disciplines) was to emphasize power relations between women and men. Authors asserted what they saw as the essential structural divisions between women and men: gender was raised to the same theoretical status as class or ethnicity. Even if this was more the 'politics of correction' rather than the 'politics of interrogation' (as Janet Wolff has described it), it was nevertheless an assertion of a form of social division (if not actual antagonism) which was regarded by many as fundamental.[6] It was sometimes the case that feminist academics came close to suggesting that before feminism there had been no politics in that academy and thus men (such as C. Wright Mills, Joseph Needham and E.J. Hobsbawm) were often marginalized, but despite this, feminists of the second wave produced work of extraordinary political vitality.

However, the question remains as to whether or not feminist theory has significantly transformed social theory. Among those most sceptical of feminism's claim to an impact on social theory is Nicos Mouzelis, who has argued that: 'While feminist theory has drawn extensively from various theoretical traditions . . . the main influence has been from theory to feminism rather than the other way round. . . . This is not surprising, since on the level of conceptual tools (Generalities II) theories tend to be quite neutral as far as gender or race is concerned . . .'[7] This assertion somewhat unequivocally resists the idea – which is essential to the understanding of culture and cultural life – that subjectivity and identity are vital components of our social reality and our social experience. Laclau and Mouffe are among those who have argued that politics should not be interpreted in terms simply of institutions but should be seen as the very form of everyday existence.[8] In that context – the discussion and the demonstration of the detail and the personal experience of social life – it is possible to list the many interventions made by feminists which have shown the difference that gender makes to social encounters and social experience. (Miriam Glucksman on time and gender is one such distinguished example.)[9] In this sense, the goal of academic feminists – to make women visible – has been achieved. It is now impossible to teach sociology without discussing gender. Whereas in 1970 class (and perhaps race) would have been deemed the most significant determinant of individual life chances and the social hierarchy, at the beginning of the twenty-first century class has to compete with gender and race for a place in the analysis of contemporary society. Again, we see sociology reflecting much that is current in ideological accounts of the social world, accounts which emphasize the centrality to experience of 'identity' politics. Despite the increase in material inequalities which occurred on both sides of the Atlantic during the 1980s, these inequalities are seldom part of current sociological considerations, except in regard to the consistent recognition that it is women who predominate in the ranks of the western poor. In Britain the decline in manufacturing industry (and the consequent destruction of many communities and the loss of many male jobs) has seldom been the subject of sociological study. Whereas once British sociology studied many traditional working-class communities, the same interest has not been sustained in the charting of the decline of those communities.[10]

Thus when Mouzelis writes about 'what went wrong' with sociological theory he directs the major weight of his criticism against Foucault, Baudrillard and other major figures of postmodernism. In these figures what he identifies as crucial is the absence of any understanding of either the meaning or the impact of social power. As he writes: 'What I exclude from sociological theory proper are "untranslated" philosophical discourses on perennial ontological/epistemological issues, as well as attempts to construct general "laws" (Generalities III) or contextless, universal generalisations, which invariably end up being wrong and/or trivial'.[11] But the theoretical tradition of Foucault *et al.*, which others as well as Mouzelis are critical of, has of course been theoretically crucial to feminism in that through 'powerlessness' (or theories about 'discursive practices') feminists have been able to identify the resistance to patriarchy which feminism always provided and to enhance and express those ideas which allow women, and the interests of women, a space in the social world. Postmodernism has been, therefore, of theoretical value to feminist academics since it provides feminism with a given theoretical legitimacy. If others (that is, male others) are 'using' the theoretical space of postmodernism then there is no reason why feminists should not have equal access to those unpoliced vistas.

Feminist sociologists have therefore very firmly placed the discussion of women and gender on the sociological agenda. The crucial question that now confronts us is that of the difference that this makes to our understanding of the central issues of sociology, and indeed to our understanding of the discipline as a whole. Those most critical of academic sociology could well argue at this point that all sociology has done in the past 30 years is continue its role as the recorder of social experience in capitalism: hence, as women have become more clearly part of the public world, sociology has duly recorded that change. This account emphasizes that descriptive quality of sociology which has always made it the easy butt of academic and literary jokes. Malcolm Bradbury's *The History Man* caught the sense that sociology could be no more than an account of the fashionable and the ephemeral: there was, in Bradbury's anti-hero Howard Kirk, no moral substance, merely an amalgam of wants and desires.[12] Bradbury's novel too easily assumed that other academic disciplines had values which were so woefully absent in sociology, but at the same time it also argued a real case against sociology, namely that it did little more than describe current mores and confused, most fundamentally, explanation with legitimation.

Bradbury, in writing *The History Man*, wrote a critique not just of sociology but of new universities in Britain in the 1960s and the emergence of a form of academic ethos rather different from that of traditional universities. His critique of sociology was not in itself novel; as already suggested a considerable tradition had challenged the idea that sociology could be 'value free' without being valueless. Feminist sociology stood within that tradition which had argued for a sociology located within a sense of values and priorities; in the case of feminism the value in question would be that of sexual equality, the argument that women, just as men, should be both subjects and objects within sociology. The study of gender is, however, more politically and morally neutral than that of the study of women. Since gender is an inescapable part of human existence, there is no intellectual or political reason to assume that its study constitutes any form of disruption of the social or the academic world.

But the title of this volume does refer to 'gender' rather than women or women's studies. It is thus that we have to ask if gender, and the study of gender, makes any difference to what might be described as the 'big issues' of sociology, the issues of class and class differences, social change and social cohesion. The first generation of second-wave academic feminists turned to Marx to argue that women, and women's unpaid labour, made possible the accumulation of surplus labour. Housework, and care for others, were universally and more or less exclusively provided by women and this work, if it did not literally make the world go round, at least ensured the maintenance of those structures which allowed paid workers to go on working. This argument suggested that the organization of gender – the social construction of the appropriate modes of femininity and masculinity – was crucial to the maintenance of both the economic and the social order of late capitalism. There were (and remain) intense skirmishes about which sex 'owns' social class and how social class and gender interrelate.[13] In this debate John Goldthorpe (and others) argued that in the majority of households, the social indicator of the life chances and the standard of living of the household was determined by the occupation of the 'primary' wage earner, which in the majority of cases was (and is) a man.[14] Notwithstanding the often stated 'fact' about the increase in the number of women in employment, the majority of employed women are in part-time work. Women's participation in the labour force remains crucially affected by the birth of children: it is certainly the case that women return to work (usually part-time work) after the birth of their first child, but with the birth of subsequent children the likelihood of women remaining in full-time employment decreases.

Despite the existence of evidence about women and paid work which suggests that women's relationship to paid work remains different from that of men, voices have for some time been raised (both literally and metaphorically) in the debate with Goldthorpe.[15] It was pointed out that many contemporary households cannot survive economically without two incomes, and that women contribute to households not just in terms of income but also in terms of aspirations and expectations. There is a case here which it is important to emphasize: namely that women in a sense 'carry' the culture of any society, and it is through women – as mothers – that children acquire their sense of expectations about the world. Literature, as well as sociology, is replete with examples of mothers who battle for the education of their children and who provide the impetus for children to succeed in education and employment. Whether or not these examples are the norm is another question: *Sons and Lovers* by D.H. Lawrence may be the definitive example in English literature of a mother determined to ensure the success of her son, but evidence abut social mobility suggests that this example was far from general. Indeed, information about social mobility in Britain (and elsewhere in the West) in the past decade suggests that there is relatively little significant social mobility and that what there is occurs either between relatively close strata of the social hierarchy or as a result of large-scale changes in the reward, status and entry structure of employment.[16] We know, for example, that many more women now enter higher education in Britain, but we also know that the numbers of either sex who enter higher education from manual or unskilled occupations remains extremely low.[17]

Thus the picture we have of society in Britain (and the USA) is one of limited social mobility: a world which, in terms of the chances of upward social mobility from the manual working class to the professional middle class is as limited now as it was 50 years ago. It is apparent that whatever else has changed in the culture of Britain and the USA, the culture of the professional middle class has remained as closed a book as it ever was to the population in general. Changes, such as the greater number of women in employment, have made little impact on the stability of the class structure – indeed, we are just as likely to marry or cohabit with people from within the boundaries of our social class as we ever were, even if we now form publicly recognized relationships between the same, as well as the different, sex. While sanctions against open premarital sexual activity have largely disappeared and cohabitation is increasingly a general experience for all social classes, this shift in sexual morality has done little to minimize the fact that changes in sexual morality are still worked out and lived out within class boundaries.

From a review of the material on class mobility and the social world of late capitalism, it is difficult to see how gender, or thinking about gender, makes a difference to the long-term structural picture of either Britain or the USA. It is the case that in both countries women constitute the majority of the poor, but women have always been among the poorest in the West, as they remain throughout the world. When sociologists speak of the 'feminization' of poverty they refuse those millions of women who for centuries lived in the most grinding and endless poverty. Precisely because norms have changed about sexual behaviour – for example the idea about 'illegitimacy' has largely disappeared from western culture – many of those women whose poverty might once have been seen as the poverty of a family (with a male unemployed breadwinner) are now 'single parents', dependent on either their own very low earnings or those of the state. It is thus important to regard critically ideas about the increase in the poverty of women:

another way of reading social information about gender and poverty would be to recognize the increase in the transparency of the poverty in which many women live. Easier divorce, remarriage and the growth of step families have allowed a greater flexibility in personal lives, but it is very often women who are the economic victims of this new moral and sexual climate, just as women were once the victims of a culture which assumed female economic dependence on men.

The failure of men to support children after divorce or separation from the mother is well known on both sides of the Atlantic and has given rise to intense debate about solutions to and causes of the phenomenon. Attempts in Britain to pursue fathers through the Child Support Agency have had limited success. Schemes in the USA to force mothers into work rather than dependence on state schemes are rightly seen as punishment of the more vulnerable.[18] In theoretical terms, evidence about men, women, children and poverty suggests that a new sexual culture has had a negative material effect upon women, even if the freedom to leave unhappy marriages or relationships is seen as positive. What remains on the political agenda of every western country is the question of how to ensure parental economic support for children. Given that the birth of children always limits the wage earning capacity of women, the relationship of the father to the child and the mother remains crucial. For many people in the West, the relationship is unproblematic. It is important to emphasize that in Britain – where the demise of the family is sometimes spoken of as achieved fact – 80 per cent of children grow up with both their natural parents. The family, and families constructed around biological parenting, has not collapsed, nor is experience of it an alien one for the majority of the population.

But cultural change, and in particular change in the way in which people think about sexual and personal morality, is making a difference to the way in which people organize their lives. Again, it is important to remember that cultural change, and change in the normative order, is not just a feature of the late twentieth and early twenty-first centuries. In the past 200 years the history of the West has been one of consistent shifts in normative assumptions. (We need only to remember that in 1960 unmarried women were expected to give away their children for adoption to see how great change in some instances has been.)[19] What is important here is the extent to which changes in gender relations, and the way we think about gender, contribute to macro social change as well as to the obvious changes that occur in individual lives. Thus we confront the issues of how change occurs in gender relations, and the part that these changes might contribute to other forms of social change. This question – of the relation between culture, society and economy – is hardly novel to sociology, but it is somewhat novel for gender to be included as a factor in the equation.

Although many feminists would contest this view, it is possible to see both first- and second-wave feminism as the protest of women against various forms of social exclusion – a reactive social movement to particular kinds of social change. In the nineteenth century, women (particularly middle-class women) fought for rights of inclusion in the civil society of industrial capitalism. In the late twentieth century, second-wave feminists fought for similar kinds of ideological and structural change: a change in the assumption that the human was synonymous with the male, and access to the public world of late capitalism on the same terms as men. (The 'same terms' included, of course, access to the same sexual morality quite as much as entry to the professions.) Feminism can thus be seen as essentially a politics of inclusion. To want to join the game, in the relationship between feminism and capitalism as elsewhere, does suggest a willingness to accept the nature of that game. Arguments against this harsh judgement invoke ideas about 'critical mass' and 'changing agendas'; arguments which suggest that the presence of numbers within institutions will effect a change.

Whether or not that is the case remains, in many instances, to be seen. So far, evidence suggests that when women come to constitute a majority in any profession or institution it loses its status and its ability to command high regard. What this does not suggest is that changes in relations between the sexes, or social expectations about gender, will significantly change or destabilize the social order as distinct from individual social experience. The culture of the social world may change, but the social order – which is that of late capitalism – remains. If we wish to argue that changes in the ordering of gender will change the social world in significant, structural ways then we have to argue in one of two ways: that women are different from men and that difference, expressed through social institutions, will effect radical social change; or that we no longer need 'gender' and are in a position to eliminate the social assumption that we need to construct femininity and/or masculinity.

The first argument owes much to radical feminism, the second to Judith Butler. The first argument, with which names as diverse as Luce Irigaray, Helene Cixous and Adrienne Rich would be associated, sees women as naturally, biologically different from men. Women's sexuality, their relationship to language and reproduction all create a sex which is fundamentally different from that of men, but has always had to live in a world organized by and for men. The second argument, essentially derived from Butler, is that creating gender creates social divisions, social needs and patterns of consumption. To eliminate gender ('doing' gender) would remove a significant force within capitalism, essentially a cultural force of constructing needs which only consumption can apparently satisfy. (For example, without the idea of feminine sexual appeal for male heterosexual men there might be no demand for the cosmetic or fashion industry, let alone cosmetic surgery.) Judith Butler might, but does not, demonstrate how many of our western industries depend upon ideas about sexual attractiveness for their driving force. The connections between high fashion and monopoly capitalism are not always immediately apparent, but they are to be made, even with a market-place which has assiduously created a multiplicity of brand names in part in order to disguise the actual simplicity of the pattern of ownership. Naomi Klein and others have observed the stranglehold which brand names have on the imagination (and the pocket) of the West, but Klein has not suggested that one sex rather than the other is beset with this determination only to consume in certain specific ways.[20]

Klein has however explained the global markets (and patterns of consumption) which now exist. In the same vein, John Urry has suggested that the traditional basis of sociology – the study of individual societies – has become outmoded in an increasingly 'borderless' world. Urry suggests that sociology has to confront the growing internationalism of the world, and sets out, in *Sociology Beyond Societies*, ideas about the implications of our present capacity both to travel literally and metaphorically.[21] It is pertinent to ask who is travelling in this new world; most evidence would seem to indicate that the rich can travel out of choice, while the poor still travel for the same reasons as ever – want, starvation and necessity. For many citizens of the West, more information about the world is available than at any time in human history, but limited knowledge and experience of social life other than the local is still the norm. Paradoxically, the country which has the greatest global influence – the USA – is also the country whose citizens have the least direct experience of cultures other than their own. It is tempting, when it is possible to buy the same commodities everywhere on the planet, to suppose that this constitutes a new world without frontiers. But to generalize about social experience on the basis of information about the distribution of commodities is problematic. In particular, while we can observe the convergence of certain patterns of social organization (for example, welfare policies in western Europe) we also have to recognize those intensely felt cultural differences which still separate individuals. Within the politics of the twenty-first century, women often become a symbol of 'progress' (whether in their inclusion in a particular institution or, more recently, where their 'emancipation' became part of the legitimation of military intervention by the USA in Afghanistan), but the terms of this symbolic construction are often those of inclusion in a western, heterosexual discourse.

Twentieth- and twenty-first-century society in the West has been viewed the most sceptically, and the most critically, by sociologists from a country which has experienced the most appalling possibilities of modern capitalism, namely Germany. In any account of social theory, the work of the Frankfurt School has to be noted for its consistent and radical critique of late capitalism. In the work of Marcuse, Horkheimer, Adorno and Benjamin there exists an account of contemporary capitalism which refuses the appeal of the apparently democratic and maintains an unshaking belief in the possibilities of the rational, rather than rationalization or the rationalizing.

These heirs of Weber and Simmel recognize – as Anglo-Saxon sociology has often failed to – that industrial capitalism can produce plenty, but to produce excellence, and to continue to be able to think critically, we need to be able to recognize the world in which we live. Unlike Giddens' idea of reflexivity, which stops short at the boundaries of the individual, the Frankfurt School stood for the recognition of the meaning of what is involved in living, and thinking, within a social system which is geared to the dual motives of profit and bureaucratic order. The School was able to recognize the distinctions made between these two pillars of social order, but what remains refreshing about their work is the clarity with which they identify the divisions between reason, profit and order.

The index of any work by any member of the Frankfurt School would reveal few citations for gender. Marcuse's *One Dimensional Man* and *Eros and Civilization* develop a thesis about sex and sexuality which might now be read as deeply reactionary, in that Marcuse refuses to accept that 'sexual liberation' is anything of the kind.[22] Indeed, Marcuse argues that eroticism has been replaced by sexualization and comes close to replicating, in relation to sexuality, Marx's description of religion as 'an opium of the people'. Sexuality – through a process of the sexualization of relationships and the growth of billion-dollar industries related to the 'sale' of sex (invariably female sexuality for the male consumer) – has become not just an aspect of the human condition but a major industry within capitalism. Marcuse's work, like that of other members of the Frankfurt School, demonstrates the author's understanding of Freud and a lack of fear about the existence and possibilities of sexuality. Precisely because Marcuse and his colleagues were able to recognize the power of sexuality, they allow ideas such as repression and collective unconscious into their world. In this they share the same recognition that is so characteristic of Simmel – that ideas about the masculine and the feminine, our fantasies about ourselves and others as sexual beings, inform our actions and understanding as social beings. For people within Anglo-Saxon traditions the idea that sexuality, as an aspect of social being rather than a private choice, is part of our social lives is deeply problematic since much of the intellectual tradition of the Anglo-Saxon academy has been organized around the idea of the human being as securely 'rational'. To bring women into this tradition was, of course, comparable to the introduction of nature into culture, particularly since women who entered the western academy in the 1970s did so as unequivocally female. Unlike previous generations, the feminist academics of second-wave feminism emphasized not their similarity with men but their difference, and the consequent difference in their interpretation of the social and intellectual world. Part of that difference has been discussed by Terry Eagleton:

> Those from the social margin are less likely to be rationalists or idealists, inflating the role of ideas. What, one might ask, have

ideas ever done for them? This is especially true of women, whose material conditions make them on the whole less spontaneously idealist than men... The German philosopher Fichte developed a theory which he named Transcendental Egoism; but as someone once observed, one would like to know what Mrs Fichte thought about that. 'He thinks, therefore she does the dirty work' would not be a bad catch-cry for feminism. Or perhaps: 'He thinks, therefore she is not allowed to'.[23]

Women have now taken a greater part in 'thinking' (in terms of involvement with the academy) than previously, even if there is little or no evidence to suggest that men do more of the 'dirty work'. Moreover, the impact of confronting the academic world with the very radical challenge to the taken for granted construction of the human subject as male has yet to be fully understood in intellectual terms. For sociology, and social theory, gender remains deeply problematic in that its impact can vary between the minimal and the absolute. Simmel was one of the first sociologists to recognize the 'feminine' quality of modernity, a recognition which Virginia Woolf was to describe in her non-fiction and to portray so vividly as the antithesis of the traditional in *Three Guineas*.[24] Woolf, like Simmel, recognized the complex constructions of masculinity and femininity. Thus Simmel, in 'Defining culture' describes women as more disposed to fidelity than men, and suggests links between this psychic inclination and the social world: 'There is something faithless in the separation of the person from the object. In this respect, it is opposed to the more constant nature of women. It estranges women – inwardly, of course – from a productive culture that is objectified on the basis of its specialisation, and specialised on the basis of its objectivity'.[25]

Woolf recognized those different relationships to the social world of women and men: men, as *Three Guineas* makes clear, created emotionally rigid institutional structures which made slaves of men themselves. The 'half man' whom Woolf pillories is a half man created from his enslavement to objective specialization. Woolf's solution to the enslavement of women and the truncated human development of men is simple: 'For if your wife were paid for her work ... your own slavery would be lightened. Work could be equally distributed. Culture would thus be stimulated. You could see the fruit trees flower in spring. You could share the prime of life with your children.[26] This visionary account of the future is as relevant today as it was in 1938, because it recognizes both the intrusion of the public onto the private sphere and, like the work of Simmel, the interplay between gender and the construction of both the private and the public. Woolf and Simmel recognize that gender socialization is not just derived from culture but endlessly constructs it. Our uncertainties about our gender continue throughout our lives and inform our social actions. As examples here it is possible to cite the part that gender played in the ideology of Fascism, as much as studies of the workplace endlessly demonstrate the way in which 'doing' gender and 'doing' work are so closely intertwined. In the case of the first example, studies such as that by Maria Macciochi have argued for the recognition of the skill with which Hitler and Mussolini managed ideas about nature and culture.[27] Equally, in her now classic study of workplace behaviour, Rosabeth Moss Kanter demonstrated that there is no such person as an employee, only a male or a female employee.[28]

What the considerable evidence about gender, and its part in the social world, now suggests is that it is impossible to study society without at the same time studying how society is constructed through expectations about male and female and masculinity and femininity. But having said that, having allowed that the construction of gender is part of our daily lives, we also have to recognize that our lives and expectations are constructed by class and race as well as gender. The question – brutally – is what affects what, and in which circumstances? For example, motherhood, unlike fatherhood, remains a social experience which has a defining impact on women's experience of the social world. So gender – in the sense that women bear children and men do not – is a crucial part of our social, as well as our personal, emotional histories. The impact of motherhood as a social rather than an emotional factor tends to diminish as children grow older and achieve some measure of independence, but (again for the majority) by that time women's integration into the workplace (in terms of skills and contacts) may have radically diminished. Whatever the efforts of governments in the West to minimize the way in which parenthood impacts on women more than men, it remains the case that motherhood is a crucial form of social division. The difficulties of uniting motherhood with paid work can be minimized for those women whose earnings are sufficient to buy effective child care, but in the main the picture of paid work for most mothers is that of a patchwork of part-time work, family assistance and some paid child care.

Motherhood as a form of social division is seldom mentioned in texts on social and sociological theory. Yet if the workplace is taken as the primary public arena of industrial capitalism, access to that place and performance within it is different for all men, for childless women and for women with children. This is a harsh division, and one which ignores those examples of striking professional success by women who have large families (Nicola Horlick of Britain, for example), or the men who abandon paid work to take up child care and household management (no famous male name occurs here quite so easily as that of Nicola Horlick). But it is a division which reflects the general picture of individual relationships to the workplace in Britain and the USA. It is by no means the absolute or the only picture, but it is a picture which reflects the general experience of the West. From information about countries other than Britain and the USA we know that the difficulty of combining paid work and motherhood has a significant impact on the birth rate. In Italy, for example, where the birth rate is well below replacement level, it is known that the reason for this is the wish of women to remain in paid work in a country where part-time work is limited and state provision for child care is minimal.[29]

Hence any account of gender and the workplace must include the recognition of the impact of motherhood on women. In Britain we know that fewer children are being born, and they are being born to older mothers. From this it is possible to conclude that the wish to remain in paid work is becoming central to all women, that participation in the workforce is now deemed an important part of adult life. At the same time it is important to ask why being in paid work is assuming central importance for women – a sexist question in itself perhaps, since it is seldom, if ever, asked of men. The answers to the question are, however, important in that they tell us much about our relationship to society. Answers must include the interest and commitment that women, just as men, have to their work; the desire to be among other people rather than in the isolation of the home; and finally (but by no means least) the need for two incomes in many households. Increasingly, in both Britain and the USA there are few households which can survive on one income; particularly in the USA, where the costs of higher education and medical care have a higher impact on household budgets than in Britain and Europe generally – remaining in the middle class is economically problematic for many US families, just as reaching it is equally difficult for blue-collar households.[30]

At this time the issue of gender and the state appears. This is not just a matter of the western state's use of women as workers in schools, hospitals and social services but also an issue of the complex relationship between the state and the relative costs of traditional and non-traditional models of femininity. The welfare state established in Britain through the Beveridge Report made no secret of the fact that it did not expect women with children to be in paid work. The role of mothers was to raise children. But the expectations of women changed, and increasingly – if implicitly rather than explicitly – western governments have found it advantageous in terms of both tax revenue and voters' expectations to modify their attitudes to working mothers. Indeed, in both Britain and the USA governments in the past five years have taken the view that mothers with children who are not supported by male partners should be in paid work. Here is a radical rethinking of social attitudes and expectations: motherhood is not to be construed as a reason for absence from paid work, and the state is not to be regarded as a surrogate husband, partner and father. Hence a situation has developed on both sides of the Atlantic where mothers who make claims on the state are no longer assumed to be justifiably absent from paid work.

This new state policy spells out to citizens (particularly female citizens) that the state does not see its function as the surrogate means of support for children without working mothers and fathers. Paid work is the place for adults in this conception of the state, regardless of individual situations. This shift in state policy accords with a general cultural shift in the West in terms of general perceptions of paid work. The shift is towards the assumption that paid work is the normal adult experience of all men (as was always the case) *and* all women. The state is in effect assisting in the growing convergence of social experience for women and men which is becoming evident in aspects of the cultural and material worlds. In saying this, it is not to deny or marginalize the fact that for many mothers the provision of state-funded child care is highly beneficial. Nor is it to deny that the personal costs for women of seclusion in the home with young children were often high. Betty Friedan, in *The Feminine Mystique*, found members of a generation of college-educated mothers going slowly crazy or becoming depressed (or both) in the suburbs of the American dream, while autobiographical accounts of growing up in the suburbs throughout the West in the 1950s paint pictures of unhappy mothers involved in bizarre, but necessary, patterns of resistance.[31] The domestic world, whether of Germaine Greer's *Daddy We Hardly Knew You*, or Carolyn Steedman's, *Landscape for a Good Woman*, or Lorna Sage's *Bad Blood*, was very far from that supposedly happy 'normality' of the advertising dream. The mothers in all these accounts of suburban domestic life were clearly less than entirely happy with their lot.[32]

Thus in noting that the western state is widely embarked upon policies which assist (or in some cases come close to coercing) mothers into paid work, it would be entirely false to suppose that the state is disturbing some Garden of Domestic Eden. Life in the family has also been beset with dangers, from the most minimally neurotic to the most literally dangerous. Generally, western populations have agreed that the state must intervene in the household in order to prevent gross poverty or gross mistreatment of women and children. This consensus has been achieved in the past 30 years at the same time as the same populations have often endorsed ideas about the illegitimate growth of state intervention in 'private' lives. The paradox is one which western governments have to negotiate, and around which they often act in contradictory directions. But in attempting to assist and intervene in the lives of citizens, western states are faced with populations which are often subject to the destabilizing impacts of changing patterns and conditions of work and ideologies which emphasize individual needs and inclinations.

In both these situations, gender plays a part. In terms of the new world of paid work it has been widely noted that it is women, rather than men, who have benefited from the development of the new service industries. The arguments need treating with scepticism, because while it is the case that much paid work in service sector occupations has been taken by women, it is often poorly paid with no career structure and considerable job insecurity.

At the same time both sexes have faced an increase in the number of white-collar jobs organized through short-term contracts or, in the public sector, levels of bureaucratic intervention and assessment which have, for many people, significantly altered the nature of the work. It is often said that the typical job of the twenty-first century is that at a 'call centre', a job in which the non-unionized worker is employed on a contract basis. This caricature does not represent the entire picture of paid work in Britain or the USA in the twenty-first century, but it does suggest that perceptions about the economic emancipation of women need to be regarded cautiously and certainly with some consideration of the nature of the social and the personal quality achieved in this emancipation. 'Job satisfaction' is highly subjective and difficult to measure, but we can deduce that paid work, which is inherently insecure, over-bureaucratized and badly paid, is unlikely to be deemed rewarding.

One of the factors which sociologists often overlook in their study of paid work is that it is an experience which is gradually involving more and more people. In the late nineteenth century it was estimated that about a quarter of the male population was unemployed in Britain; male unemployment remained a political issue throughout the twentieth century and it is apparent that female unemployment is beginning to be deemed socially significant. Being in employment remains, for the great majority of the male population, both economically and socially preferable to unemployment and increasingly this is the case for women. Moreover, there is a sense in which western societies equate effective citizenship with the effective ability to consume. To be without access to an income has never been desirable, poverty has always been a form of social exclusion, but contemporary poverty excludes not just in the ancient material sense, but also excludes from participation in the myths and fantasies created by society. To go shopping, to inhabit the cosmopolitan urban world of the twenty-first century, demands money and that sense of personal autonomy which money makes possible.

The past 30 years have seen the growing integration of women into the normative structure of late capitalism, an integration which is no longer expressed through male relatives or partners, but directly by individual women themselves. Women, as Marx predicted, have been brought into the social world through their entry into production. What has, however, not yet occurred in any visible form is the contribution of this integration to a social radicalism which is the precursor for socialism. It is true that those women who continue to vote in the West vote more often for parties of the political left than for the political right, but to translate the 'gender gap' in British or US politics as part of the first step towards socialism or radical social transformation would be wildly premature. What we need to ask, however unwillingly, is whether the changing position of women makes any real difference to the structure and the continuity of western capitalism. It is demonstrable that the economic emancipation of women has not been accompanied by any substantial shifts in the organization of the household or the gender of the sex which holds significant political and economic power. Barriers to the further emancipation of women clearly remain in certain spheres, but the extent to which changes in the position of women create social tensions to which the social world cannot adapt remains questionable, as does Gidddens' thesis that what he sees as new forms of heterosexual emotional relationships will extend democracy.

Perhaps more problematic – and certainly perceived as more problematic in certain political quarters – is not the extension of the integration of women into the normative framework of late capitalism, but what is constructed as the 'flight' of young men from it. Moral panics have emerged in Britain about the growing success of girls in secondary education: success which not only matches that of men but overtakes them. Those most beset by panic can gain some reassurance from the fact that while girls may outperform boys, young men outperform young women. For example, considerable energy has been devoted to the finding, at the University of Cambridge, that young men consistently gain higher classes of degree than women. The explanation for this is that what this examination rewards is intellectual aggression and what is perceived by examiners (the majority of them male) as 'originality'; in other words, what has been described by Val Walsh as 'the virility culture'.[33] What is less often rewarded is the careful consideration of evidence and the ability to see different points of view – characteristics which are associated with women.

In a context which is of limited general relevance we confront issues about nature and nurture: have women been trained and socialized into, if not a passive acceptance of the world then at least a less confrontational attitude to it? The past century has seen the gradual acceptance of the idea, throughout most of the world, that the 'getting of wisdom' should be allowed to both women and men. But women's involvement and engagement with 'knowledge' remains complicated (like that of men) by ideas about the implications of the agency which knowledge involves and allows. Women have gained access to previously male institutions of knowledge, but it is difficult to perceive that as yet these structures (like those of the world of paid work or politics) are radically altered by shifts in their gender composition. As Frantz Fanon has pointed out in another context, the excluded can take on the worst characteristics of their oppressors; in the context of feminism, bell hooks and Audrey Lorde have been among those who have agreed with Fanon that, in Lorde's phrase, 'the master's tools will never dismantle the master's house'.[34]

So far, therefore, the entry of women into the public world offers little sign of having a destabilizing impact. But when young men appear to be abandoning interest in the public world and conventional expectations of masculinity, there is concern across the political spectrum. Barbara

Ehrenreich – on the left of politics in the USA – has identified what she sees as men's flight from the 'breadwinner' model. The sexualization of western culture in the 1960s and 70s brought with it, she argued, a shift in male values from those which saw prestige and status in the male ability to support a family to a society in which men were judged more in terms of their ability to be sexually attractive to women rather than their ability to provide domestic support. The encouragement of emotional expressiveness in men – an idea very often supported by women – brought with it expectations which very often undermined women's interests. The rewriting of the western script about gender, in which what is described as 'emotional literacy' is as much valued in men as in women, is possibly more disruptive of our expectations about social order than any of the other social and ideological changes that have occurred in the past 40 years. (The previous 'mis-treating' of men, and the social refusal of men's capacity for empathy, have been noted by R.W. Connell and Caroline New).[35] The disruption lies in the possible erosion of the culture of the Protestant ethic, an ethic which for the past 500 years has provided the West with cohesion and social energy. Men's participation in this ethic (whether forced or voluntary) provided capitalism with a generally cooperative workforce, while gender differentiation allowed both cultural and social specializations. The gradual disappearance – certainly since the 1960s – of gender differentiation in cultural forms and practices has created a social world which is arguably more socially rather than materially unstable than in the past. Our capacity to produce goods is unparalleled, but our capacity to maintain a degree of social order and creativity is arguably diminished by the disappearance of gender differentiation. Gender differences always played their part in offering alternatives to the relentless pursuit of the capitalist ethic, in that femininity stood for ideals of care while masculinity stood for equally transcendent ideals of justice and liberty – precisely that intense loyalty to individuals and that objectivity which Simmel identified.

Capitalism was made by men, with the unquestioning assumption that women – dominated by nature – would remain in a distinct and separate space, providing support for the activities of men. Generations of women have questioned aspects of male behaviour and male constructions of knowledge and the social world. For many people in the West, the twenty-first century has eroded expectations about gender which segregated the sexes and defined them in culturally distinct ways. What remains, and what remains as an issue for social theory, is the relationship between people – particularly women – and children. We are now offered what is in effect an androgynous world, a world in which the impact of class and race remains but that of gender has considerably lessened. But that androgyny collapses immediately in the face of an event which remains largely that of nature: the birth of children. Current social policies in parts of the West, and progressive politics in much of it, are attempting to abolish the idea (although not the substance) of motherhood and replace it with parenthood. For ideological and economic reasons there is much resistance to this idea, but should it be achieved the twenty-first century could see the emergence of a world in which gender has very little social significance. This is not to suggest that gender difference will disappear, but that its impact on social experience may become limited. What will remain, as Marx predicted, will be a world of class difference, in which the culture produced by late capitalism will have brought about that transparency of class differences which previous cultures could not achieve. When both sexes are integrated into the social world, then the construction of that social world may become more clearly that of differences between classes rather than women and men. The relevance of gender, not just to social theory but to our experience of the social world, may thus not increase, but diminish.

In conclusion, therefore, and as a response to the question about the impact of a discussion of gender on social theory, it is useful to cite a quotation from Max Weber:

> Not ideas, but material and ideal interests, directly govern men's conduct. Yet very frequently the 'world images' that have been created by 'ideas' have, like switchmen, determined the tracks along which action has been pushed by the dynamic interest. 'From what' and 'for what' one wished to be redeemed and, let us not forget 'could' be redeemed, depended upon one's image of the world.[36]

The 'world images' which are currently created in the West are predominantly those of entitlement and individualism, and there is little evidence to suggest that the sexes participate differentially in the internationalization and the acceptance of these normative patterns. It is apparent that women in the West are now allowed (and claim) greater individual agency and autonomy than in previous historical periods, but this shift – while individually emancipating – is not necessarily socially disruptive. The politics of feminism which have shifted diverse social practices towards women depend – as Max Weber pointed out – on one's image of the world. The images of the world which we have do not, I would argue, emerge exclusively from our gender or our understanding of it: men and women are both capable of political choices which transcend gender and it is in that context – in terms of choices between entitlement and enlightenment, collectivism and individualism – that gender difference both dissolves and yet remains a crucial aspect of the human condition. We cannot (yet) be human without a gender identity, but we cannot fulfil our humanity without a recognition of the limitations, as well as the strengths, of that identity.

NOTES

Chapter 1   Enter women

1 Michele Barrett (1992) Words and things: materialism and method in contemporary feminist analysis', in Michele Barrett and Anne Phillips, *Destabilizing Theory: Contemporary Feminist Debates*, pp. 201–20 (Cambridge: Polity Press).

2 Marshall Berman (1983) *All That is Solid Melts into Air: The Experience of Modernity* (London: Verso).

3 Vikki Bell (1999) *Feminist Imagination* (London: Sage); Dorothy Smith (1987) *The Everyday World as Problematic: A Feminist Sociology* (Boston, MA: North Eastern University); Sylvia Walby (1990) *Theorising Patriarchy* (Oxford: Blackwell); Sarah Franklin, Celia Lury and Jackie Stacey (2000) *Global Nature, Global Culture* (London: Sage).

4 Anthony Giddens (1992) *The Transformation of Intimacy* (Cambridge: Polity Press); Stevi Jackson (1993) Even sociologists fall in love: an exploration in the sociology of emotions, *Sociology*, 27(2): 201–20; Simon Williams (1998) Emotions in social life, in Gillian Bendelow and Simon Williams (eds) *Emotions in Social Life*, pp. xv–xxx (London: Routledge).

5 Max Weber (1958) *The Protestant Ethic and the Spirit of Capitalism* (New York: Charles Scribner).

6 Beverley Skeggs (1997) *Formations of Class and Gender* (London: Sage).

7 See Virginia Woolf (1993) *The Crowded Dance of Modern Life* (London: Penguin) and the discussion about Woolf and modernity in John Jervis (1998) *Exploring the Modern*, pp. 261–2 (Oxford: Blackwell).

8 Virginia Woolf ([1929] 1992) *A Room of One's Own*, (Oxford: Oxford University Press).

9 Marion Milner (1987) *The Suppressed Madness of Sane Men* (London: Tavistock).

10 Ann Oakley (1972) *Sex Gender and Society* (London: Temple Smith).

11 Sheila Rowbotham, Sally Alexander and Barbara Taylor (1981) Sexual politics, in Raphael Samuel (ed.) *People's History and Socialist Theory*, pp. 364–74 (London: Routledge & Kegan Paul).

12 Mary Evans (1991) The problem of gender for women's studies, in Jane Aaron and Sylvia Walby (eds) *Out of the Margins*, pp. 67–75 (London: Falmer).

13 Marlene Le Gates (2001) *In Their Time: A History of Feminism in Western Society*, pp. 197–280 (London: Routledge).

14 Philip Larkin (1988) Annus Mirabilis ('Sexual intercourse began/in 1963') in *Collected Poems*, p. 167 (London: Faber & Faber).

15 Sylvia Plath (1966) *The Bell Jar* (London: Faber & Faber).

16 Ibid. p. 85.

17 Betty Friedan (1963) *The Feminine Mystique* (London: Penguin).

18 Shulamith Firestone (1971) *The Dialectic of Sex* (New York: Bantam); Sheila Rowbotham (1973) *Hidden from History* (London: Pluto); Kate Millett (1977) *Sexual Politics* (London: Virago); Germaine Greer (1971) *The Female Eunuch* (London: MacGibbon & Kee).

19 Martha Nussbawm (1999) The professor of parody, *New Republic*, 22 February: 1.

20 Joanne de Groot (1997) After the ivory tower, *Feminist Review*, 55(Spring): 130–142.

21 Georg Simmel (1986) Soziologie der sinne, quoted in David Frisby and Derek Sayer, *Society* (London: Tavistock).

22 Philip Larkin (1988) Self's the Man, in *Collected Poems*, p. 117 (London: Faber & Faber).

23 Ann Oakley (1974) *The Sociology of Housework* (London: Martin Robertson); Ann Oakley (1974) *Housewife* (London: Allen Lane).

24 Hannah Gavron (1966) *The Captive Wife* (London: Routledge & Kegan Paul).

25 Arlie Hochschild (1997) *The Time Bind: When Work Becomes Home and Home Becomes Work* (New York: Henry Holt); Richard Scase (2000) *Britain in 2010* (Oxford: Capstone).

26 Robert Putnam (2000) *Bowling Alone* (New York: Simon & Schuster); Richard Sennett (1998) *The Corrosion of Character* (New York: Norton).

27 George Orwell *Nineteen Eighty-Four* ([1994] 1989) (London: Penguin); Max Weber (1967) Politics as a vocation, in H.H. Gerth and C.W. Mills (eds) *From Max Weber*, p. 128 (London: Routledge & Kegan Paul).

28 Pamela Abbott and Clare Wallace (1997) *An Introduction to Sociology: Feminist Perspectives*, p. 18 (London: Routledge).

29 Simone de Beauvoir ([1949] 1986) *The Second Sex* (London: Penguin).

30 Judith Butler (1998) Merely cultural, *New Left Review*, 227(January/February): 42.

31 Nancy Fraser (1997) Heterosexism, misrecognition and capitalism: a response to Judith Butler, *Social Text*, 52–3(Fall/Winter).

32 Plato (1961) *The Republic*, p. 149 (Oxford: Oxford University Press).

33 Londa Scheibinger (1989) *The Mind has no Sex* (Cambridge, MA: Harvard University Press).

34 Jane Austen ([1818] 1965) *Persuasion*, p. 237 (London: Penguin).

35 F. Hegel ([1821] 1974) *The Philosophy of Right* (The Hague: Martin Nijhoff).

36 Simone de Beauvoir, op. cit. p. 741.

37 Emile Durkheim (1968) *The Division of Labour in Society*, p. 59 (New York: Free Press).

38 Ibid. p. 60.

39 Ibid. p. 61.
40 Georg Simmel (1984) The problem of the sexes, in G. Oakes (ed.) *Georg Simmel: On Women, Sexuality and Love*, p. 103 (New Haven, CT: Yale University Press).
41 Henrietta Moore (1994) *A Passion for Difference* (Cambridge: Polity Press); Luce Irigaray (1981) The sex which is not one, in Elaine Marks and Isabelle de Courtivron (eds) *New French Feminisms*, p. 105 (Brighton: Harvester).
42 Kate Millett quoted in Janet Sayers (1982) *Biological Politics*, p. 1 (London: Tavistock).
37 Adrienne Rich (1977) *Of Woman Born* (London: Virago).
38 Kate Soper (1990) Feminism, humanism and postmodernism, *Radical Philosophy*, 55(Summer): 14.

Chapter 2   The meaning of work

1 Among the most interesting accounts of social theory are Anthony Giddens (1992) *Capitalism and Modern Social Theory* (Cambridge: Cambridge University Press); Larry Ray (1999) *Theorizing Classical Sociology* (Buckingham: Open University Press), Anne Witz (2001) George Simmel and the masculinity of modernity, *Journal of Classical Sociology*, 1(3): 353–70; Barbara Marshall (1994) *Engendering Modernity: Feminism, Social Theory and Social Change* (Oxford: Oxford University Press).
2 Nancy Armstrong (1987) *Desire and domestic Fiction: A Political History of the Novel*, p. 35 (Oxford: Oxford University Press).
3 Sandra Harding (1991) *Whose Science? Whose Knowledge? Thinking from Women's Lives* (Buckingham: Open University Press); Donna Haraway (1989) *Primate Visions: Gender, Race and Nature in the World of Modern Science* (New York: Routledge); Hilary Rose (1994) *Love, Power and Knowledge*, (Cambridge: Polity Press); Sarah Franklin *Embodied Progress: A Cultural Account of Assisted Conception* (London: Routledge).
4 Mary Wollstonecraft ([1792] 1970) *A Vindication of the Rights of Women* (London: Dent).
5 Ibid. p. 3.
6 Hugh Cunningham (2001) *The Challenge of Democracy* (London: Longman).
7 Gillian Beer (1998) Introduction to Mary Shelley, *Frankenstein*, p. xxxv (Oxford: Oxford University Press).
8 Ibid.
9 Zygmunt Baumann (1991) *Modernity and the Holocaust* (Cambridge: Polity Press).
10 Theodor Adorno (1974) *Minima Moralia* (London: LLB).
11 Sarah Franklin (1977) *Embodied Progress: A Cultural Account of Assisted Conception* (London: Routledge) and Dolly: a new form of transgenic breedwealth, *Environmental Values*, 6(4): 427–37.
12 Nancy Armstrong, op. cit. p. 8.
13 Michel Foucault (1997) *The Archaeology of Knowledge* (London: Routledge).
14 Catherine Belseym (1991) Afterword: a future for materialist-feminist criticism? in Valerie Wayne (ed.) *The Matter of Difference: Materialist-Feminist Criticism of Shakespeare*, p. 262 (Ithaca, NY: Cornell University Press).

15 See Maxine Molyneux (1979) Beyond the housework debate, *New Left Review*, 116(July/August): 3–27.
16 Michele Barrett (1984) Introduction to Freidrich Engels, *The Origin of the Family, Private Property and the State*, p. 26 (London: Penguin).
17 Veronica Beechey (1986) Studies of women's employment, in *Feminist Review* (ed.) *Waged Work: A Reader*, pp. 130–59 (London: Virago) and Hilary Wainwright (1987) The limits of laborism, *New Left Review*, 164: 34–50.
18 See Sonia Kruks, Rayna Rapp and Marilyn Young (eds) (1989) *Promissory Notes: Women in the Transition to Socialism* (New York: Monthly Review Press).
19 Barbara Einhorn (1993) *Cinderella Goes to Market: Citizenship, Gender and Women's Movements in East Central Europe* (London: Virago).
20 Irene Bruegel (1986) The reserve army of labour, in *Feminist Review* (ed.), *Waged Work: A Reader*, pp. 40–53 (London: Virago).
21 The interpretation offered, for example, by Bruegel, ibid.
22 Christine Delphy (1977) *The Main Enemy: A Materialist Analysis of Women's Oppression* (London: WRRC Publications) and Michele Barrett and Mary McIntosh (1979) Christine Delphy: towards a materialist feminism?', *Feminist Review*, 1: 95–106.
23 E.J. Hobsbawm (1975) *The Age of Capital, 1848–1875*, p. 3 (London: Weidenfeld & Nicolson).
24 See A. Posadskaya (ed.) *Women in Russia: A New Era in Russian Feminism* (London: Verso).
25 Karl Marx (1964) *The Economic and Philosophic Manuscripts of 1844*, p. 151 (New York: International Publishers).
26 Hilary Land (1978) Who cares for the family? *Journal of Social Policy*, 7(3): 257–84; Hilary Graham (1983) Caring: a labour of love, in J. Finch and D. Groves (eds) *A Labour of Love: Women Work and Caring* (London: Routledge & Kegan Paul); Clare Ungerson (1987) *Policy is Personal* (London: Tavistock).
27 Louis Althusser (1970) *Reading Capital* (London: Verso); Juliet Mitchell (1974) *Psychoanalysis and Feminism* (London: Allen Lane).
28 David Harvey (1989) *The Condition of Postmodernity*, p. 49 (Oxford: Blackwell).
29 Works by Pierre Bourdieu include *Distinction: A Social Critique of the Judgement of Taste* (London, Routledge, 1986) and *Practical Reason* (Cambridge, Polity Press, 1998). Beverley Skeggs discusses Bourdieu in *Formations of Class and Gender* (London: Sage, 1997) as does Terry Lovell in 'Thinking feminism with and against Bourdieu', in *Feminist Theory*, 1(1): 11–32.
30 Francis Fukuyama (1997) The end of history?, *National Interest*, 16: 5–18.
31 Beatrix Campbell (1993) *Goliath: Britain's Dangerous Places* (London: Methuen); Susan Faludi (1999) *Stiffed: The Betrayal of the Modern Man* (London: Chatto & Windus).
32 See C. Skelton (1998) Feminism and research into masculinities and schooling, *Gender and Education*, 10: 217–28; W. Parkin (1993) The public and the private: gender, sexuality and emotion, in S. Fineman (ed.) *Emotion in Organisation*, pp. 167–89 (London: Sage).
33 Sally Alexander (1976) Women's work in nineteenth century London: a study of the years 1820–1850, in Ann Oakley and Juliet Mitchell (eds) *The Rights and*

Wrongs of Women, pp. 59–112 (London: Penguin); and Angela John (1984) *By the Sweat of their Brow: Women Workers at Victorian Coal Mines* (London: Routledge & Kegan Paul).

34 See, for example, S. Avineri (1968) *The Social and Political Thought of Karl Marx* (Cambridge: Cambridge University Press) and H. Lefebvre (1968) *The Sociology of Marx* (London: Penguin).

35 This is particularly apparent in Lukacs' challenge to Stalinism, *The Historical Novel* (London: Merlin, 1962).

36 Karl Marx, op. cit. p. 167.

37 Jay Dixon (1999) *The Romance Fiction of Mills and Boon, 1909–1990s* (London: University College Press).

38 Judith Butler (1990) *Gender Trouble* (London: Routledge).

39 See, for example, Lisa Adkins (1995) *Gendered Work: Sexuality, Family and the Labour Market* (Buckingham: Open University Press) and Rosemary Crompton (1999) *Restructuring Gender Relations and Employment* (Oxford: Oxford University Press).

40 Paul Willis (1977) *Learning to Labour* (Farnborough: Saxon House); Huw Beynon (1975) *Working for Ford* (Wakefield: EP Publishing); N. Dennis, F. Henriques and C. Slaughter (1969) *Coal is our Life* (London: Tavistock).

41 Marie Jahoda, Paul Lazarsfeld and Hans Zeisel, (1972) *Marienthal: The Sociology of an Unemployed Community* (London, Tavistock).

42 George Orwell *Coming up for Air* ([1939] 1962) (London:); Sinclair Lewis (1922) *Babbitt* (New York: Harcourt Brace).

43 Rosemary Pringle (1990) *Secretaries Talk: Sexuality, Power and Work* (London: Verso); Miriam Glucksmann (1990) *Women Assemble: Women Workers and the New Industries in Inter-war Britain* (London: Routledge).

44 C.W. Mills (1959) *The Power Elite* (New York: Oxford University Press); John Urry and John Wakeford (eds) (1973) *Power in Britain* (London: Heinemann).

45 Richard Hoggart (1958) *The Uses of Literacy* (London: Penguin).

46 Arlie Hochschild (1997) *The Time Bind* (New York: Metropolitan Books) and *The Second Shift: Working Parents and the Revolution at Home* (New York: Viking).

Chapter 3   The world of intimacy

1 Anthony Giddens (1992) *The Transformation of Intimacy* (Cambridge: Polity Press).

2 See John Jervis (1998) *Exploring the Modern*, p. 326 (Oxford: Blackwell); Lynn Jamieson (1999) Intimacy transformed? A critical look at the 'pure relationship', *Sociology*, 33(3): 477–94.

3 See, for example, Gordon Hughes and Ross Ferguson (eds) *Ordering Lives: Family, Work and Welfare* (London: Routledge).

4 Mike Savage (1992) Women's expertise, men's authority, in Mike Savage and Anne Witz (eds) *Gender and Bureaucracy*, p. 146 (Oxford: Blackwell).

5 Gillian Youngs (2000) Breaking patriarchal bonds, in Marianne Marchand and Anne Sisson Runyan (eds) *Gender and Global Restructuring*, pp. 44–58 (London: Routledge).

6 Scott Lash (1990) *The Sociology of Postmodernism*, p. 11 (London: Routledge).

7 John Jervis, op. cit. p. 324.

8 Max Weber (1958) *The Protestant Ethic and the Spirit of Capitalism*, p. 117 (New York: Charles Scribner).

9 Ulrick Beck and Elisabeth Beck-Gernsheim (1995) *The Normal Chaos of Love* (Cambridge: Polity Press).

10 Mirra Komarovsky (1946) Cultural contradictions and sex roles, *American Journal of Sociology*, 52(November): 184–9.

11 Betty Friedan (1963) *The Feminine Mystique* (London: Penguin); Hannah Gavron (1966) *The Captive Wife* (London: Routledge & Kegan Paul); Ann Oakley (1974) *Housewife* (London: Allen Lane); Ann Oakley (1974) *The Sociology of Housework* (London: Martin Robertson).

12 For example, Cynthia Fuchs Epstein (1970) *Women's Place: Options and Limits in Professional Careers* (Berkeley, CA: University of California Press).

13 Juliet Mitchell (1966) The long revolution, *New Left Review*, 40(November/December): 11–37; Sheila Rowbotham (1973) *Woman's Consciousness, Man's World* (London: Penguin).

14 See Chapter 2, n. 22 and Diana Leonard and Lisa Adkins (eds) (1996) *Sex in Question: French Materialist Feminism* (London: Taylor & Francis).

15 See Elaine Marks and Isabelle de Courtivron (eds) (1981) *New French Feminisms* (Brighton: Harvester).

16 Simone de Beauvoir (1986) *The Second Sex*, p. 727 (London: Penguin).

17 Hélène Cixous (1981) The laugh of the Medusa, in Elaine Marks and Isabelle Courtivron (eds) op. cit. pp. 245–64.

18 Adrienne Rich (1977) *Of Woman Born* (London: Virago); Adrienne Rich (1980) Compulsory heterosexuality and lesbian existence, *Signs*, 5(4): 631–60.

19 John Jervis, op. cit. p. 327.

20 Michel Foucault (1980) Truth and power, in C. Gordon (ed.) *Michel Foucault: Power/Knowledge*, pp. 109–33 (Brighton: Harvester); Jean-Francois Lyotard (1984) *The Post Modern Condition* (Madison, MN: Minnesota University Press).

21 An outstanding re-writing of the history of sexuality, much influenced by Foucault, was Jeffrey Weeks (1981) *Sex, Politics and Society: The Regulation of Sexuality Since 1800* (Harlow: Longman).

22 Paul Gilroy (1996) *The Black Atlantic: Modernity and Double Consciousness* (London: Verso); Stuart Hall (1990) Culture, identity and diaspora, in J. Rutherford (ed.) *Identity: Community, Culture and Difference* (London: Lawrence & Wishart); Edward Said (1994) *Culture and Imperialism* (London: Vintage).

23 Maggie Humm (1991) *Border Traffic: Strategies of Contemporary Women Writers* (Manchester: Manchester University Press).

24 Liz Stanley and Sue Wise (1983) *Breaking Out: Feminist Consciousness and Feminist Research* (London: Routledge & Kegan Paul).

25 C.W. Mills (1959) *The Sociological Imagination* (New York: Oxford University Press).

26 Nancy Hartsock (1987) The feminist standpoint, in Sandra Harding (ed.) *Feminism and Methodology*, pp. 157–80 (Milton Keynes: Open University Press).

27 Caroline Ramazanoglu (ed.) (1993) *Up Against Foucault: Explorations of Some Tensions Between Foucault and Feminism* (London: Routledge).

28 Joan Scott (1988) *Gender and the Politics of History* (New York: Columbia University Press).

29 Sylvia Walby (1997) *Gender Transformations*, p. 212 (London: Routledge).
30 Marilyn Strathern (1997) 'Improving ratings': audit in the British university system', *European Review*, 5(3): 305–21.
31 Max Weber (1967) Bureaucracy, in H. Gerth and C. Wright Mills (eds) *From Max Weber*, p. 243 (London: Routledge & Kegan Paul).
32 John Jervis, op. cit. p. 336.
33 Beverley Skeggs (1997) *Formations of Class and Gender*, p. 166 (London: Sage).
34 Terry Lovell (2000) Thinking feminism with and against Bourdieu, *Feminist Theory*, 1(1): 25.
35 Jane Lewis, with Jessica Datta and Sophie Sarre (1999) *Individualism and Commitment in Marriage and Cohabitation*, p. 89 (London: Lord Chancellor's Department).
36 Catherine Hakim (1996) *Key Issues in Women's Work: Female Heterogeneity and the Polarisation of Women's Employment* (London: Athlone Press).
37 Rosemary Crompton and Fiona Harris (1998) Explaining women's employment patterns: 'orientations to work revisited', *British Journal of Sociology*, 49(1): 118–36.
38 John Holmwood (2001) Gender and critical realism: a critique of Sayer; Andrew Sayer (2001) Reply to Holmwood, *Sociology*, 35(4): 981.

Chapter 4   The gendered self

1 Carole Pateman (1988) *The Sexual Contract* (Cambridge: Polity Press).
2 Jean Elshtain (1981) *Public Man, Private Woman: Women in Social and Political Thought* (Princeton, NL: Princeton University Press); Irene Bruegel (1979) Women as a reserve army of labour: a note on recent British experience, *Feminist Review*, 3: 12–23; Veronica Beechey (1977) Some notes on female wage labour in capitalist production, *Capital and Class*, 3: 45–66; Susan Himmelweit (1984) The real dualism of sex and class, *Review of Radical Political Economics*, 16(1): 167–83; Ann Oakley (1972) *Sex, Gender and Society* (London: Martin Robertson); Sheila Allen (1982) Gender inequality and class formation, in A. Giddens and G. Mackenzie (eds) *Social Class and the Division of Labour* (Cambridge: Cambridge University Press); Margaret Stacey and Marion Price (1981) *Women, Power and Politics* (London: Tavistock).
3 Simone de Beauvoir (1986) *The Second Sex*, p. 16 (London: Penguin).
4 Toril Moi (1994) *Simone de Beauvoir: The Making of an Intellectual Woman* (Oxford: Blackwell); Sonia Kruks (1988) Simone de Beauvoir: between Sartre and Merleau-Ponty, *Simone de Beauvoir Studies*, 5: 74–80; Judith Butler (1990) *Gender Trouble*, pp. 10–12 and 111–12 (London: Routledge); Vickki Bell (1999) *Feminist Imagination* (London: Sage).
5 Simone de Beauvoir, op. cit. p. 295.
6 Sonia Kruks (2001) *Retrieving Experience. Subjectivity and Recognition in Feminist Politics*, p. 51 (Ithaca, NY: Cornell University Press).
7 Judith Butler, op. cit.
8 Ibid. p. 148.
9 Ibid. p. 149.

10 Nancy Fraser (1998) Heterosexist capitalism? *New Left Review*, March/April: 140–9; Martha Nussbawm (1999) The professor of parody, *The New Republic*, February: 1–21.

11 Nancy Fraser, op. cit. p. 147.

12 Mike Brake (1976) I may be queer, but at least I am a man, in D. Barker and S. Allen (eds) *Dependence and Exploitation in Work and Marriage* (London: Longman).

13 Judith Butler (1999) *Excitable Speech: A Politics of the Performative* (London: Routledge).

14 Martha Nussbawm, op. cit. p. 18.

15 Evidence about attitudes to, and behaviour within, marriage is assessed in Jane Lewis, Jessica Datta and Sophie Sarre (1999) *Individualism and Commitment in Marriage and Cohabitation* (London: Lord Chancellor's Department).

16 Catherine Hakim (1995) Five feminist myths about women's employment, *British Journal of Sociology*, 46(3): 429–55.

17 Jane Humphries (1981) Protective legislation, the capitalist state and working class men: the case of the 1842 Mines Regulation Act, *Feminist Review*, 7: 1–33.

18 Hilary Land (1980) The family wage, *Feminist Review*, 6: 55–77.

19 Penny Sommerfield (1984) *Women Workers in the Second World War: Production and Patriarchy in Conflict*, p. 185 (London: Routledge).

20 Ibid. p. 187.

21 Claudia Koonz (1988) *Mothers in the Fatherland: Women, the Family and Nazi Politics* (London: Methuen).

22 Vicky Randall and Georgina Waylen (1998) *Gender Politics and the State* (London: Routledge).

23 Jean Blondel (1963) Towards a general theory of change in voting behaviour, *Political Studies*, 13: 93–5.

24 Sheila Allen (1999) Gender inequality and divisions of labour, in Huw Beynon and Pandeli Glavanis (eds) *Patterns of Social Inequality*, pp. 20–35 (London: Longman).

25 Linda McDowell (1997) *Capital Cultures* (Oxford: Blackwell).

26 Barbara Ehrenreich (1989) *Fear of Falling: The Inner Life of the Middle Class* (New York: Pantheon).

27 Richard Titmuss and Katherine Titmuss (1942) *Parents Revolt: A Study of the Declining Birthrate in Acquisitive Societies* (London: Secker & Warburg); A.J.P. Taylor (1965) *English History, 1914–1945*, p. 301 (Oxford: Clarendon Press).

28 Richard Sennett (1998) *The Corrosion of Character: The Personal Consequences of Work in the New Capitalism* (London: Norton); Barbara Ehrenreich (1989) *Fear of falling* (New York: Pantheon).

29 Philip Brown (2000) The globalization of positional competition? *Sociology*, 34(4): 633–53.

30 Annie Phizacklea and Carol Wolkowitz (1998) *Homeworking Women: Gender, Racism and Class at Work* (London: Sage); Sallie Westwood and Parminder Bhachu (1988) *Enterprising Women* (London: Routledge).

31 Nancy Chodorow (1978) *The Reproduction of Mothering* (Berkeley, CA: University of California Press).

32 Henrietta Moore (1996) Mothering in a cross-cultural perspective, in Elizabeth Bortolaia Silva (ed.) *Good Enough Mothering?* pp. 58–75 (London: Routledge).
33 Beverley Skeggs (1997) *Formations of Class and Gender*, p. 161 (London: Sage).
34 Karl Marx and Friedrich Engels (1958) *Selected Works*, vol. 1, p. 363 (Moscow: Foreign Language Publishing House).
35 Raymond Williams (1973) *The Country and the City* (London: Chatto & Windus); Terry Eagleton (1988) *Myths of Power: A Marxist Study of the Brontës* (Basingstoke: Macmillan).
36 Michele Barrett and Anne Phillips (eds) (1992) *Destabilising Theory* (Cambridge: Polity Press).
37 Andrew Sayer (2001) Reply to Holmwood, *Sociology*, 35(4): 980.

Chapter 5 The real world

1 Zygmunt Banmann (1991) *Modernity and the Holocaust* (Cambridge: Polity Press).
2 John Jervis (1998) *Exploring the Modern*, p. 230 (Oxford: Blackwell).
3 Ibid. p. 233.
4 Ann Douglas (1977) *The Feminization of American Culture* (New York: Alfred Knopf); Elaine Showalter (1992) *Sexual Anarchy: Gender and Culture at the Fin de Siécle* (London: Virago); Alice Jardine (1985) *Gynesis: Configurations of Woman and Modernity* (Ithaca, NY: Cornell University Press).
5 Virginia Woolf (1928) *Orlando* (London: Hogarth Press).
6 Virginia Woolf ([1938] 1992) *Three Guineas*, p. 356 (Oxford: Oxford University Press).
7 Ibid. p. 364.
8 Virginia Woolf ([1929] 1992) *A Room of One's Own* (Oxford: Oxford University Press); John Maynard Keynes (1919) *The Economic Consequences of the Peace* (London: Macmillan).
9 George Ritzer (1996) *The McDonaldization of Society: An Investigation into the Changing Character of Contemporary Social Life* (London: Sage).
10 Herbert Marcuse (1964) *One Dimensional Man* (London: Routledge & Kegan Paul); Jurgen Habermas (1989) *The Structural Transformation of the Cultural Sphere: An Inquiry into a Category of Bourgeois Society* (Cambridge: Polity Press); Francis Fukuyama (1997) The end of history?, *National Interest*, 16: 5–18.
11 E.J. Hobsbawm (1996) The cult of identity politics, *New Left Review*, 217(May/June): 38–47.
12 Lucien Goldmann (1970) Les deux avant-gardes, in *Structures Mentales et Création Culturelle*, p. 184 (Paris: Anthropos).
13 Nigel Thrift (1999) Capitalism's cultural turn, in Larry Ray and Andrew Sayer (eds) *Culture and Economy after the Cultural Turn* (London: Sage).
14 Stuart Hall (1988) Brave new world, *Marxism Today*, 24 October: 24–9.
15 For an account of the work of the Frankfurt School see Martin Jay (1973) *The Dialectical Imagination* (London: Heinemann).
16 Richard Hoggart (1958) *The Uses of Literacy* (London: Penguin).
17 Ralph Samuel (1994) *Theatres of Memory* (London: Verso); *Island Stories* (London: Verso).

18 Mirra Komarovsky (1946) Cultural contradictions and sex roles, *American Journal of Sociology*, 52(3): 184–9.

19 Scott Lash (1990) *The Sociology of Postmodernism*, p. 11 (London: Routledge).

20 Anne Phillips and Barbara Taylor (1986) Sex and skill, in *Feminist Review* (ed.) *Waged Work*, pp. 55–65.

21 Jenny Uglow (1987) George Eliot and the woman question, in *George Eliot*, pp. 65–81 (London: Virago).

22 Sue Lees (1993) *Sugar and Spice: Sexuality and Adolescent Girls* (London: Penguin); Michelle Fine and Pat Macpherson (1994) Over dinner: feminism and adolescent female bodies', in H.L. Radtke and H.J. Stam (eds) *Power/Gender: Social Relations in Theory and Practice*, pp. 219–47. (London: Sage).

23 Elizabeth Wilson, Bohemian love, in Mike Featherstone (ed.) *Love and Eroticism*, pp. 111–28 (London: Sage).

24 Mary Mellor (1962) *Feminism and Ecology* (Cambridge: Polity Press); Rachel Carson (1962) *Silent Spring* (London: Penguin).

25 Marlene Le Gates (2001) *In Their Time: A History of Feminism in Western Society* (London: Routledge).

26 Lorna Sage (2000) *Bad Blood* (London: Fourth Estate).

27 Ibid. p. 186.

28 Valerie Walkerdine and Helen Lucey (1989) *Democracy in the Kitchen: Regulating Mothers and Socialising Daughters* (London: Virago).

29 Barbara Rogers (1980) *The Domestication of Women* (London: Tavistock).

30 Michele Barrett and Mary McIntosh (1982) *The Anti-social Family* (London: Verso); David Cooper (1971) *The Death of the Family* (London: Penguin); R.D. Laing (1976) *The Politics of the Family* (London: Penguin); R.D. Laing and Aaron Esterson (1999) *Sanity, Madness and the Family* (London: Routledge).

31 Philip Larkin (1988) This Be the Verse, in *Collected Poems*, p. 180 (London: Faber & Faber).

32 Beveridge Report (1942) *Report on Social Insurance and Allied Services*, Cmnd.6404 (London: HMSO).

33 Viola Klein (1946) *The Feminine Character* (London: Routledge & Kegan Paul).

34 Adrienne Rich (1980) Compulsory heterosexuality and lesbian existence, *Signs*, 5(4): 631–60.

35 Michel Foucault (1981) *The History of Sexuality* (London: Penguin).

36 Ken Plummer (ed.) (1968) *The Making of the Modern Homosexual* (London: Hutchinson); Mary McIntosh (1978) Who needs prostitutes? The ideology of male sexual needs, in Carol Smart and Barry Smart (eds) *Women, Sexuality and Social Control* (London: Routledge & Kegan Paul); Jeffrey Weeks (1981) *Sex, Politics and Society* (London: Longman).

37 Cas Wouters (1998) Sex and love since the 1960s sexual revolution, in *Theory, Culture and Society*, 15(3–4): 187–214.

38 Juliet Mitchell (1974) *Psychoanalysis and Feminism* (London: Allen); Carol Gilligan (1982) *In A Different Voice* (Boston, MA: Harvard University Press).

39 Jacqueline Rose (1986) *Sexuality in the field of Vision* (London: Verso); Terry Castle (1993) *The Apparitional Lesbian* (New York: Columbia University Press).

40 Kathy Davis (1992) Toward a feminist rhetoric: Gilligan debate revisited, *Women's Studies International Forum*, 15(1): 219–31; Nancy Coney and Wade

Mackey (1997) A reexamination of Gilligan's analysis of the female moral system: distaff altruism will not succeed, *Human Nature*, 8(3): 247–73.

41 John Berger (1977) *Ways of Seeing* (London: Penguin).

42 Catherine MacKinnon (1989) *Towards a Feminist Theory of the State* (Cambridge: Harvard University Press); Andrea Dworkin (1981) *Pornography: Men Possessing Women* (London: Women's Press); Sheila Jeffreys (1990) *Anticlimax: A Feminist Perspective on the Sexual Revolution* (London: The Women's Press).

43 Sue Lees (1986) *Losing Out* (London: Hutchinson).

44 Michelle Fine (1988) Sexuality, schooling and adolescent females: the missing discourse of desire, *Harvard Educational Review*, 58(1): 29–53.

45 Jeffrey Weeks (1998) The sexual citizen, *Theory Culture and Society*, 15(3–4): 35–52.

46 Elizabeth Wilson (1997) Saint Diana, *New Left Review*, 226(November/December): 136–45.

47 Robert Fernquist and Phillips Cutright (1998) Societal integration and age standardised suicide rates in 21 developed countries, *Social Science Research*, 27(2): 109–27.

48 Susan Bordo (1993) Unbearable Weight: *Feminism, Western Culture and the Body* (Berkeley, CA: University of California Press).

49 Emile Durkheim (1970) *Suicide: A Study in Sociology* (London: Routledge).

Chapter 6   Now you see it, now you don't

1 Alvin Gouldner (1971) *The Coming Crisis of Western Sociology* (London: Heinemann).

2 C.W. Mills (1967) The professional ideology of social pathologists, in *Power, Politics and People*, p. 538 (Oxford: Oxford University Press).

3 Orlando Figes (1996) *A People's Tragedy* (London Pimlico).

4 Bob Jessop (1997) Capitalism and its future: remarks on regulation, government and governance, *Review of International Political Economy*, 4: 361–81.

5 Nicos Mouzelis (1991) *Back to Sociological Theory: The Construction of Social Orders* (London: Macmillan) and (1995) *Sociological Theory: What Went Wrong* (London: Routledge); Anthony Giddens (1998) *The Third Way: The Renewal of Social Democracy* (Cambridge: Polity Press).

6 Janet Wolff (2000) The feminine in modern art: Benjamin Simmel and the gender of modernity, *Theory, Culture and Society*, 17(6): 33–53.

7 Nicos Mouzelis (1996) After postmodernism: a reply to Gregor McLennan, *Sociology*, 30(1): 132.

8 E. Laclau and C. Mouffe (1985) *Hegemony and Socialist Strategy: Towards a Radical Democratic Politics* (London: Verso).

9 Miriam Glucksman (1998) What a difference a day makes: a theoretical and historical explanation of temporality and gender, *Sociology*, 32(2): 239–58.

10 For example, Brian Jackson (1972) *Working Class Community* (London: Pelican).

11 Nicos Mouzelis, op. cit. p. 134.

12 Malcolm Bradbury (1975) *The History Man* (London: Secker & Warburg).

13 Kenneth Prandy and Robert Blackburn (1997) Putting men and women into classes: but is that where they belong?, *Sociology*, 31(1): 143–52.

14 Geoffrey Evans (1996) Putting men and women into classes: an assessment of the cross-sex validity of the Goldthorpe class schema, *Sociology*, 30(2): 209–34.
15 Hakon Leiulfsrud and Alison Woodward (1987) Repudiating conventional theories of family class, *Sociology*, 21(3): 393–412.
16 Robert Erikson and John Goldthorpe (1993) *The Constant Flux: A Study of Class Mobility in Industrial Societies* (Oxford: Oxford University Press).
17 Sheila Jacobs (1999) Trends in women's career patterns and in gender occupational mobility in Britain, *Gender, Work and Organisation*, 6(1): 32–46.
18 Simon Duncan and Rosalind Edwards (1999) *Lone Mothers, Paid Work and Gendered Rationalities* (Basingstoke: Macmillan).
19 Ann Phoenix (1996) Social constructions of lone motherhood: a case of competing discourses, in Elizabeth Bortolaia Silva (ed.) *Good Enough Mothering? Feminist Perspectives on Lone Motherhood*, pp. 175–90 (London: Routledge).
20 Naomi Klein (2000) *No Logo* (London: Flamingo).
21 John Urry (2000) *Sociology Beyond Societies* (London: Routledge).
22 Herbert Marcuse (1956) *Eros and Civilization* (London: Routledge & Kegan Paul) and (1964) *One Dimensional Man* (London: Routledge & Kegan Paul).
23 Terry Eagleton (2001) *The Gatekeeper: A Memoir*, pp. 56–8 (London: Penguin).
24 Virginia Woolf ([1938] 1992) *Three Guineas* (Oxford: Oxford University Press).
25 Georg Simmel (1997) Defining culture' in David Frisby and Mike Featherstone (eds) *Simmel on Culture*, p. 51 (London: Sage).
26 Virginia Woolf, op. cit. p. 317.
27 Maria-Antonietta Macciochi (1979) Female sexuality in Fascist ideology, *Feminist Review*, 1: 67–82.
28 Rosabeth Moss Kanter (1977) *Men and Women of the Corporation* (New York: Basic Books).
29 R. Lorenzo (1993) *Italy: Too Little Time and Space for Childhood* (Florence: UNICEF).
30 Barbara Ehrenreich (1989) *Fear of Falling: The Inner Life of the Middle Class* (New York: Pentheon).
31 Betty Friedan (1983) *The Feminine Mystique* (London: Pelican).
32 Germaine Greer (1990) *Daddy We Hardly Knew You* (London: Penguin); Carolyn Steedman (1986) *Landscape for a Good Woman* (London: Virago). Lorna Sage (2000) *Bad Blood* (London: Fourth Estate).
33 Val Walsh (1994) Virility culture, in Mary Evans, Juliet Gosling and Anne Seller (eds) *Agenda for Gender* (Canterbury: Centre for Women's Studies, University of Kent at Canterbury).
34 Frantz Fanon (1968) *Black Skin, White Masks* (London: MacKibbon and Kee); bell hooks, *Outlaw Culture* (London: Routledge); Andre Lorde (1984) The master's tools will never dismantle the master's house, in *Sister Outsider*, pp. 110–13 (Trumansburg, NY: Crossing Press).
35 R.W. Connell (1995) *Masculinities* (Cambridge: Polity Press); Caroline New (2001) Oppressed and oppressors? *Sociology*, 35(3): 729–48.
36 Max Weber (1948) Social psychology of world religions' in H. Gerth and C.W. Mills (eds) *From Max Weber*, p. 280 (London: Routledge & Kegan Paul).

BIBLIOGRAPHY

Aaron, J. and Walby, S. (eds) (1991) *Out of the Margins*. London: Falmer.

Abbott, P. and Wallace, C. (1997) *An Introduction to Sociology: Feminist Perspectives*. London: Routledge.

Adkins, L. (1995) *Gendered Work: Sexuality, Family and the Labour Market*. Buckingham: Open University Press.

Adorno, T. (1974) *Minima Moralia*. London: LLB.

Althusser, L. (1970) *Reading Capital*. London: Verso.

Armstrong, N. (1987) *Desire and Domestic Fiction: A Political History of the Novel*. Oxford: Oxford University Press.

Austen, J. ([1818] 1965) *Persuasion*. London: Penguin.

Avineri, S. (1968) *The Social and Political Thought of Karl Marx*. Cambridge: Cambridge University Press.

Barker, D. and Allen, S. (eds) (1976) *Dependence and Exploitation in Work and Marriage*. London: Longman.

Barrett, M. and McIntosh, M. (1979) Christine Delphy: towards a materialist feminism? *Feminist Review*, 1: 95–106.

Barrett, M. and McIntosh, M. (1982) *The Anti-social Family*. London: Verso.

Barrett, M. and Phillips, A. (eds) (1992) *Destabilizing Theory: Contemporary Feminist Debates*. Cambridge: Polity Press.

Baumann, Z. (1991) *Modernity and the Holocaust*. Cambridge: Polity Press.

Beck, U. and Beck-Gernsheim, E. (1995) *The Normal Chaos of Love*. Cambridge: Polity Press.

Beechey, V. (1977) Some notes on female wage labour in capitalist production, *Capital and Class*, 3: 45–66.

Bell, V. (1999) *Feminist Imagination*. London: Sage.

Bendelow, G. and Williams, S. (eds) (1998) *Emotions in Social Life*. London: Routledge.

Berger, J. (1977) *Ways of Seeing*. London: Penguin.

Berman, M. (1983) *All That is Solid Melts into Air: The Experience of Modernity*. London: Verso.

Beveridge Report (1942) *Report on Social Insurance and Allied Services*, Cmnd 6404. London: HMSO.

Beynon, H. (1975) *Working for Ford*. Wakefield: E.P. Publishing.

Beynon, H. and Glavanis, P. (eds) *Patterns of Social Inequality*. London: Longman.

Blondel, J. (1963) Towards a general theory of change in voting behaviour, *Political Studies*, 13: 93–5.

Bordo, S. (1993) *'Unbearable Weight': Feminism, Western Culture and the Body*. Berkeley, CA: University of California Press.

Bortolaia, E.S. (ed.) (1996) *Good Enough Mothering?* London: Routledge.

Bourdieu, P. (1986) *Distinction: A Social Critique of the Judgement of Taste*. London: Routledge.

Bourdieu, P. (1998) *Practical Reason*. Cambridge: Polity Press.

Bradbury, M. (1975) *The History Man*. London: Secker & Warburg.

Brown, P. (2000) The globalization of positional competition? *Sociology*, 34(4): 633–53.

Bruegel, I. (1979) Women as a reserve army of labour: a note on recent British experience, *Feminist Review*, 3: 12–23.

Butler, J. (1990) *Gender Trouble*. London: Routledge.

Butler, J. (1998) Merely cultural, *New Left Review*, 227(January/February): 42.

Butler, J. (1999) *Excitable Speech: A Politics of the Performative*. London: Routledge.

Campbell, B. (1993) *Goliath: Britain's Dangerous Places*. London: Methuen.

Carson, R. (1962) *Silent Spring*. London: Penguin.

Castle, T. (1993) *The Apparitional Lesbian*. New York: Columbia University Press.

Chodorow, N. (1978) *The Reproduction of Mothering*. Berkeley, CA: University of California Press.

Coney, N. and Mackey, W. (1997) A reexamination of Gilligan's analysis of the female moral system: distaff altruism will not succeed, *Human Nature*, 8(3): 247–73.

Connell, R.W. (1995) *Masculinities*. Cambridge: Polity Press.

Cooper, D. (1971) *The Death of the Family*. London: Penguin.

Crompton, R. (1999) *Restructuring Gender Relations and Employment*. Oxford: Oxford University Press.

Crompton, R. and Harris, F. (1998) Explaining women's employment patterns: 'orientations to work' revisited, *British Journal of Sociology*, 49(1): 118–36.

Cunningham, H. (2001) *The Challenge of Democracy*. London: Longman.

Davis, K. (1992) Toward a feminist rhetoric: Gilligan debate revisited, *Women's Studies International Forum*, 15(1): 219–31.

de Beauvoir, S. ([1949] 1983) *The Second Sex*. London: Penguin.

de Groot, J. (1997) After the ivory tower, *Feminist Review*, 55(spring): 130–42.

Delphy, C. (1977) *The Main Enemy: A Materialist Analysis of Women's Oppression*. London: WRRC Publications.

Dennis, N., Henriques, F. and Slaughter, C. (1969) *Coal is our Life*. London: Tavistock.

Dixon, J. (1999) *The Romance Fiction of Mills and Boon, 1909–1990s*. London: University College Press.

Douglas, A. (1977) *The Feminization of American Culture*. New York: Alfred Knopf.

Duncan, S. and Edwards, R. (1999) *Lone Mothers, Paid Work and Gendered Rationalities*. Basingstoke: Macmillan.

Durkheim, E. (1968) *The Division of Labour in Society*. New York: Free Press.

Durkheim, E. (1970) *Suicide: A Study in Sociology*. London: Routledge.

Dworkin, A. (1981) *Pornography: Men Possessing Women*. London: Women's Press.
Eagleton, T. (1988) *Myths of Power: A Marxist Study of the Brontës*. Basingstoke: Macmillan.
Eagleton, T. (2001) *The Gatekeeper: A Memoir*. London: Penguin.
Ehrenreich, B. (1989) *Fear of Falling: The Inner Life of the Middle Class*. New York: Pantheon.
Einhorn, B. (1993) *Cinderella Goes to Market: Citizenship, Gender and Women's Movements in East Central Europe*. London: Virago.
Elshtain, J. (1981) *Public Man, Private Woman: Women in Social and Political Thought*. Princeton, NJ: Princeton University Press.
Engels, F. (1984) *The Origin of the Family, Private Property and the State*. London: Penguin.
Epstein, C.F. (1970) *Women's Place: Options and Limits in Professional Careers*. Berkeley, CA: University of California Press.
Erikson, R. and Goldthorpe, J. (1993) *The Constant Flux: A Study of Class Mobility in Industrial Societies*. Oxford: Oxford University Press.
Evans, G. (1996) Putting men and women into classes: an assessment of the cross-sex validity of the Goldthorpe class schema, *Sociology*, 30(2): 209–34.
Evans, M., Gosling, J. and Seller, A. (eds) *Agenda for Gender*. Canterbury: Centre for Women's Studies, University of Kent at Canterbury.
Faludi, S. (1999) *Stiffed: The Betrayal of the Modern Man*. London: Chatto & Windus.
Fanon, F. (1968) *Black Skin, White Masks*. London: MacKibbon & Kee.
Featherstone, M. (ed.) (1999) *Love and Eroticism*. London: Sage.
Feminist Review (ed.) (1986) *Waged Work: A Reader*. London: Virago.
Fernquist, R. and Cutright, P. (1998) Societal integration and age standardised suicide rates in 21 developed countries, *Social Science Research*, 27(2): 109–27.
Figes, O. (1996) *A People's Tragedy*. London: Pimlico.
Finch, J. and Groves, D. (eds) (1983) *A Labour of Love: Women Work and Caring*. London: Routledge & Kegan Paul.
Fine, M. (1988) Sexuality, schooling and adolescent females: the missing discourse of desire, *Harvard Educational Review*, 58(1): 29–53.
Firestone, S. (1971) *The Dialectic of Sex*. New York: Bantam.
Foucault, M. (1981) *The History of Sexuality*. London: Penguin.
Foucault, M. (1997) *The Archaeology of Knowledge*. London: Routledge.
Franklin, S. (1977) *Embodied Progress: A Cultural Account of Assisted Conception*. London: Routledge.
Franklin, S. (1997) Dolly: a new form of transgenic breedwealth, *Environmental Values*, 6(4): 427–37.
Franklin, S., Lury, C. and Stacey, J. (2000) *Global Nature, Global Culture*. London: Sage.
Fraser, N. (1997) Heterosexism, misrecognition and capitalism: a response to Judith Butler, *Social Text*, Fall/Winter: 52–3.
Fraser, N. (1998) Heterosexist capitalism?, *New Left Review*, March/April: 140–9.
Friedan, B. (1963) *The Feminine Mystique*. London: Penguin.
Frisby, D. and Sayer, D. (1986) *Society*. London: Tavistock.
Frisby, D. and Featherstone, M. (eds) (1997) *Simmel on Culture*. London: Sage.
Fukuyama, F. (1997) The end of history? *National Interest*, 16: 5–18.

Gavron, H. (1966) *The Captive Wife.* London: Routledge & Kegan Paul.

Gerth, H.H. and Mills, C.W. (eds) (1967) *From Max Weber.* London: Routledge & Kegan Paul.

Giddens, A. (1992) *Capitalism and Modern Social Theory.* Cambridge: Cambridge University Press.

Giddens, A. (1992) *The Transformation of Intimacy.* Cambridge: Polity Press.

Giddens, A. (1998) *The Third Way: The Renewal of Social Democracy.* Cambridge: Polity Press.

Giddens, A. and Mackenzie, G. (eds) (1982) *Social Class and the Division of Labour.* Cambridge: Cambridge University Press.

Gilligan, C. (1982) *In A Different Voice.* Cambridge, MA: Harvard University Press.

Gilroy, P. (1996) *The Black Atlantic: Modernity and Double Consciousness.* London: Verso.

Glucksmann, M. (1990) *Women Assemble: Women Workers and the New Industries in Inter-war Britain.* London: Routledge.

Glucksman, M. (1998) What a difference a day makes: a theoretical and historical explanation of temporality and gender, *Sociology,* 32(2): 239–58.

Goldmann, L. (1970) Les deux avant-gardes, in *Structures Mentales et Création Culturelle.* Paris: Anthropos.

Gordon, C. (ed.) (1980) *Michel Foucault: Power/Knowledge.* Brighton: Harvester.

Gouldner, A. (1971) *The Coming Crisis of Western Sociology.* London: Heinemann.

Greer, G. (1971) *The Female Eunuch.* London: MacGibbon & Kee.

Greer, G. (1990) *Daddy We Hardly Knew You.* London: Penguin.

Habermas, J. (1989) *The Structural Transformation of the Cultural Sphere: An Inquiry into a Category of Bourgeois Society.* Cambridge: Polity Press.

Hakim, C. (1995) Five feminist myths about women's employment, *British Journal of Sociology,* 46(3): 429–55.

Hakim, C. (1996) *Key Issues in Women's Work: Female Heterogeneity and the Polarisation of Women's Employment.* London: Athlone Press.

Hall, S. (1988) Brave new world, *Marxism Today,* 24 October: 24–9.

Haraway, D. (1989) *Primate Visions: Gender, Race and Nature in the World of Modern Science.* New York: Routledge.

Haraway, D. (1991) *Simians, Cyborgs and Women: The Reinvention of Nature.* London: Free Association Books.

Harding, S. (ed.) (1987) *Feminism and Methodology.* Milton Keynes: Open University Press.

Harding, S. (1991) *Whose Science? Whose Knowledge? Thinking from Women's Lives.* Buckingham: Open University Press.

Harvey, D. (1989) *The Condition of Postmodernity.* Oxford: Blackwell.

Hegel, F. ([1821] 1974) *The Philosophy of Right.* The Hague: Martinus Nijhoff.

Himmelweit, S. (1984) The real dualism of sex and class, *Review of Radical Political Economics,* 16(1): 167–83.

Hobsbawm, E.J. (1975) *The Age of Capital, 1848–1875.* London: Weidenfeld & Nicolson.

Hobsbawm, E.J. (1996) The cult of identity politics, *New Left Review,* 217(May/June): 38–47.

Hochschild, A. (1989) *The Second Shift: Working Parents and the Revolution at Home.* New York: Viking.

Hochschild, A. (1997) *The Time Bind: When Work Becomes Home and Home Becomes Work*. New York: Henry Holt.

Hoggart, R. (1958) *The Uses of Literacy*. London: Penguin.

Holmwood, J. (2001) Gender and critical realism: a critique of Sayer, *Sociology*, 35(4): 981.

hooks, b. (1994) *Outlaw Culture*. London: Routledge.

Hughes, G. and Ferguson, R. (eds) (2000) *Ordering Lives: Family, Work and Welfare*. London: Routledge.

Humm, M. (1991) *Border Traffic: Strategies of Contemporary Women Writers*. Manchester: Manchester University Press.

Humphries, J. (1981) Protective legislation, the capitalist state and working class men: the case of the 1842 Mines Regulation Act, *Feminist Review*, 7: 1–33.

Jackson, B. (1972) *Working Class Community*. London: Pelican.

Jackson, S. (1993) Even sociologists fall in love: an exploration in the sociology of emotions, *Sociology*, 27(2): 201–20.

Jacobs, S. (1999) Trends in women's career patterns and in gender occupational mobility in Britain, *Gender, Work and Organisation*, 6(1): 32–46.

Jahoda, M., Lazarsfeld, P. and Zeisel, H. (1972) *Marienthal: The Sociology of an Unemployed Community*. London: Tavistock.

Jamieson, L. (1999) Intimacy transformed? A critical look at the 'pure relationship', *Sociology*, 33(3): 477–94.

Jardine, A. (1985) *Gynesis: Configurations of Woman and Modernity*. Ithaca, NY: Cornell University Press.

Jay, M. (1973) *The Dialectical Imagination*. London: Heinemann.

Jeffreys, S. (1990) *Anticlimax: A Feminist Perspective on the Sexual Revolution*. London: The Women's Press.

Jervis, J. (1998) *Exploring the Modern*. Oxford: Blackwell.

Jessop, B. (1997) Capitalism and its future: remarks on regulation, government and governance, *Review of International Political Economy*, 4: 361–81.

John, A. (1984) *By the Sweat of their Brow: Women Workers at Victorian Coal Mines*. London: Routledge & Kegan Paul.

Kanter, R.M. (1977) *Men and Women of the Corporation*. New York: Basic Books.

Keynes, J.M. (1919) *The Economic Consequences of the Peace*. London: Macmillan.

Klein, N. (2000) *No Logo*. London: Flamingo.

Klein, V. (1946) *The Feminine Character*. London: Routledge & Kegan Paul.

Komarovsky, M. (1946) Cultural contradictions and sex roles, *American Journal of Sociology*, 52(3): 184–9.

Koonz, C. (1988) *Mothers in the Fatherland: Women, the Family and Nazi Politics*. London: Methuen.

Kruks, S. (1988) Simone de Beauvoir: between Sartre and Merleau-Ponty, *Simone de Beauvoir Studies*, 5: 74–80.

Kruks, S. (2001) *Retrieving Experience: Subjectivity and Recognition in Feminist Politics*. Ithaca, NY: Cornell University Press.

Kruks, S., Rapp, R. and Young, M. (eds) (1989) *Promissory Notes: Women in the Transition to Socialism*. New York: Monthly Review Press.

Laclau, E. and Mouffe, C. (1985) *Hegemony and Socialist Strategy: Towards a Radical Democratic Politics*. London: Verso.

Laing, R.D. (1976) *The Politics of the Family*. London: Penguin.

Laing, R.D. and Esterson, A. (1999) *Sanity, Madness and the Family*. London: Routledge.

Land, H. (1978) Who cares for the family? *Journal of Social Policy*, 7(3): 257–84.

Land, H. (1980) The family wage, *Feminist Review*, 6: 55–77.

Larkin, P. (1988) *Collected Poems*. London: Faber & Faber.

Lash, S. (1990) *The Sociology of Postmodernism*. London: Routledge.

Le Gates, M. (2001) *In Their Time: A History of Feminism in Western Society*. London: Routledge.

Lees, S. (1986) *Losing Out*. London: Hutchinson.

Lees, S. (1993) *Sugar and Spice: Sexuality and Adolescent Girls*. London: Penguin.

Lefebvre, H. (1968) *The Sociology of Marx*. London: Penguin.

Leiulfsrud, H. and Woodward, A. (1987) Repudiating conventional theories of family class, *Sociology*, 21(3): 393–412.

Leonard, D. and Adkins, L. (eds) (1996) *Sex in Question: French Materialist Feminism*. London: Taylor & Francis.

Lewis, J. with Datta, J. and Sarre, S. (1999) *Individualism and Commitment in Marriage and Cohabitation*. London: Lord Chancellor's Department.

Lewis, S. (1922) *Babbitt*. New York: Harcourt Brace.

Lorde, A. (1984) *Sister Outsider*. Trumansburg, NY: Crossing Press.

Lorenzo, R. (1993) *Italy: Too Little Time and Space for Childhood*. Florence: UNICEF.

Lovell, T. (2000) Thinking feminism with and against Bourdieu, *Feminist Theory*, 1(1): 11–32 and 25.

Lukacs, G. (1962) *The Historical Novel*. London: Merlin.

Lyotard, J-F. (1984) *The Post Modern Condition*. Madison, MN: Minnesota University Press.

Macciochi, M-A. (1979) Female sexuality in Fascist ideology, *Feminist Review*, 1: 67–82.

MacKinnon, C. (1989) *Towards a Feminist Theory of the State*. Cambridge, MA: Harvard University Press.

Marchand, M. and Sisson Runyan, A. (eds) *Gender and Global Restructuring*. London: Routledge.

Marcuse, H. (1956) *Eros and Civilization*. London: Routledge & Kegan Paul.

Marcuse, H. (1964) *One Dimensional Man*. London: Routledge & Kegan Paul.

Marks, E. and de Courtivron, I. (eds) (1981) *New French Feminisms*. Brighton: Harvester.

Marshall, B. (1994) *Engendering Modernity: Feminism, Social Theory and Social Change*. Oxford: Oxford University Press.

Marx, K. (1964) *The Economic and Philosophic Manuscripts of 1844*. New York: International Publishers.

Marx, K. and Engels, F. (1958) *Selected Works*, vol. 1. Moscow: Foreign Language Publishing House.

McDowell, L. (1997) *Capital Cultures*. Oxford: Blackwell.

Mellor, M. (1997) *Feminism and Ecology*. London: Polity Press.

Millett, K. (1977) *Sexual Politics*. London: Virago.

Mills, C.W. (1959) *The Power Elite*. New York: Oxford University Press.

Mills, C.W. (1959) *The Sociological Imagination*. New York: Oxford University Press.

Mills, C.W. (1967) *Power, Politics and People*. Oxford: Oxford University Press.

Milner, M. (1987) *The Suppressed Madness of Sane Men*. London: Tavistock.

Mitchell, J. (1966) The long revolution, *New Left Review*, 40(November/December): 11–37.

Mitchell, J. (1974) *Psychoanalysis and Feminism*. London: Allen Lane.

Moi, T. (1994) *Simone de Beauvoir: The Making of an Intellectual Woman*. Oxford: Blackwell.

Molyneux, M. (1979) Beyond the housework debate, *New Left Review*, 116(July/August): 3–27.

Mouzelis, N. (1991) *Back to Sociological Theory: The Construction of Social Orders*. London: Macmillan.

Mouzelis, N. (1995) *Sociological Theory: What Went Wrong*. London: Routledge.

Mouzelis, N. (1996) After postmodernism: a reply to Gregor McLennan, *Sociology*, 30(1): 132.

New, C. (2001) Oppressed and oppressors? *Sociology*, 35(3): 729–48.

Nussbawm, M. (1999) The professor of parody, *The New Republic*, February: 1–21.

Oakes, G. (ed.) (1984) *Georg Simmel: On Women, Sexuality and Love*. New Haven, CT: Yale University Press.

Oakley, A. (1972) *Sex Gender and Society*. London: Temple Smith.

Oakley, A. (1974) *Housewife*. London: Allen Lane.

Oakley, A. (1974) *The Sociology of Housework*. London: Martin Robertson.

Oakley, A. and Mitchell, J. (eds) (1976) *The Rights and Wrongs of Women*. London: Penguin.

Orwell, G. ([1939] 1962) *Coming up for Air*. London: Penguin.

Orwell, George ([1949] 1989) *Nineteen Eighty-Four*. London: Penguin.

Paruin, W. (1993) The public and the private: gender, sexuality and emotion, in S. Fineman (ed.) *Emotion in Organisation*, pp. 167–89. London: Sage.

Pateman, C. (1988) *The Sexual Contract*. Cambridge: Polity Press.

Phizacklea, A. and Wolkowitz, C. (1995) *Homeworking Women: Gender, Racism and Class at Work*. London: Sage.

Plath, S. (1966) *The Bell Jar*. London: Faber & Faber.

Plato (1961) *The Republic*. Oxford: Oxford University Press.

Plummer, K. (ed.) (1968) *The Making of the Modern Homosexual*. London: Hutchinson.

Posadskaya, A. (ed.) (1994) *Women in Russia: A New Era in Russian Feminism*. London: Verso.

Prandy, K. and Blackburn, R. (1997) Putting men and women into classes: but is that where they belong? *Sociology*, 31(1): 143–52.

Pringle, R. (1989) *Secretaries Talk: Sexuality, Power and Work*. London: Verso.

Putnam, R. (2001) *Bowling Alone*. New York: Touchstone.

Radtke, H.L. and Stam, H.J. (eds) (1994) *Power/Gender: Social Relations in Theory and Practice*. London: Sage.

Ramazanoglu, C. (ed.) (1993) *Up Against Foucault: Explorations of Some Tensions between Foucault and Feminism*. London: Routledge.

Randall, V. and Waylen, G. (1998) *Gender Politics and the State*. London: Routledge.

Ray, L. (1999) *Theorising Classical Sociology*. Buckingham: Open University Press.

Ray, L. and Sayer, A. (eds) (1999) *Culture and Economy after the Cultural Turn.* London: Sage.

Rich, A. (1977) *Of Woman Born.* London: Virago.

Rich, A. (1980) Compulsory heterosexuality and lesbian existence, *Signs*, 5(4): 631–60.

Ritzer, G. (1996) *The McDonaldization of Society: An Investigation into the Changing Character of Contemporary Social Life.* London: Sage.

Rogers, B. (1980) *The Domestication of Women.* London: Tavistock.

Rose, H. (1994) *Love, Power and Knowledge.* Cambridge: Polity Press.

Rose, J. (1986) *Sexuality in the field of Vision.* London: Verso.

Rowbotham, S. (1973) *Hidden from History.* London: Pluto.

Rowbotham, S. (1973) *Woman's Consciousness, Man's World.* London: Penguin.

Rutherford, J. (ed.) (1990) *Identity: Community, Culture and Difference.* London: Lawrence & Wishart.

Sage, L. (2000) *Bad Blood.* London: Fourth Estate.

Said, E. (1994) *Culture and Imperialism.* London: Viutage.

Samuel, R. (1994) *Theatres of Memory.* London: Verso.

Samuel, R. (1998) *Island Stories.* London: Verso.

Samuel, R. (ed.) (1981) *People's History and Socialist Theory.* London: Routledge & Kegan Paul.

Savage, M. and Witz, A. (eds) (1992) *Gender and Bureaucracy.* Oxford: Blackwell.

Sayer, A. (2001) Reply to Holmwood, *Sociology*, 35(4): 978.

Sayers, J. (1982) *Biological Politics.* London: Tavistock.

Scase, R. (2000) *Britain in 2010.* Oxford: Capstone.

Scheibinger, L. (1989) *The Mind has no Sex.* Cambridge, MA: Harvard University Press.

Scott, J. (1988) *Gender and the Politics of History.* New York: Columbia University Press.

Sennett, R. (1998) *The Corrosion of Character: The Personal Consequences of Work in the New Capitalism.* London: Norton.

Shelley, M. ([1818] 1998) *Frankenstein: the Modern Prometheus.* Oxford: Oxford University Press.

Showalter, E. (1992) *Sexual Anarchy: Gender and Culture at the Fin de Siécle.* London: Virago.

Silva, E.B. (ed.) (1996) *Good Enough Mothering? Feminist Perspectives on Lone Motherhood.* London: Routledge.

Skeggs, B. (1997) *Formations of Class and Gender.* London: Sage.

Skelton, C. (1998) Feminism and research into masculinities and schooling, *Gender and Education*, 10: 217–28.

Smart, C. and Smart, B. (eds) (1978) *Women, Sexuality and Social Control.* London: Routledge & Kegan Paul.

Smith, D. (1987) *The Everyday World as Problematic: A Feminist Sociology.* Boston, MA: North Eastern University.

Sommerfield, P. (1984) *Women Workers in the Second World War: Production and Patriarchy in Conflict.* London: Routledge.

Soper, K. (1990) Feminism, humanism and postmodernism, *Radical Philosophy*, 55(summer): 11–17.

Stacey, M. and Price, M. (1981) *Women, Power and Politics.* London: Tavistock.

Stanley, L. and Wise, S. (1983) *Breaking Out: Feminist Consciousness and Feminist Research*. London: Routledge & Kegan Paul.

Steedman, C. (1986) *Landscape for a Good Woman*. London: Virago.

Strathern, M. (1997) 'Improving ratings': audit in the British university system, *European Review*, 5(3): 305–21.

Taylor, A.J.P. (1965) *English History, 1914–1945*. Oxford: The Clarendon Press.

Titmuss, R. and Titmuss, K. (1942) *Parents Revolt: A Study of the Declining Birthrate in Acquisitive Societies*. London: Secker & Warburg.

Uglow, J. (ed.) (1987) *George Eliot*. London: Virago.

Ungerson, C. (1987) *Policy is Personal*. London: Tavistock.

Urry, J. (2000) *Sociology Beyond Societies*. London: Routledge.

Urry, J. and Wakeford, J. (eds) (1973) *Power in Britain*. London: Heinemann. Wainwright, H.

Walby, S. (1990) *Theorising Patriarchy*. Oxford: Blackwell.

Walby, S. (1997) *Gender Transformations*. London: Routledge.

Walkerdine, V. and Lucey, H. (1989) *Democracy in the Kitchen: Regulating Mothers and Socialising Daughters*. London: Virago.

Wayne, V. (ed.) (1991) *The Matter of Difference: Materialist-Feminist Criticism of Shakespeare*. Ithaca, NY: Cornell Univrsity Press.

Weber, M. (1958) *The Protestant Ethic and the Spirit of Capitalism*. New York: Charles Scribner.

Weeks, J. (1998) The sexual citizen, *Theory Culture and Society*, 15(3–4): 35–52.

Weeks, J. (1981) *Sex, Politics and Society: The Regulation of Sexuality Since 1800*. Harlow: Longman.

Westwood, S. and Bhachu, P. (1988) *Enterprising Women*. London: Routledge.

Williams, R. (1973) *The Country and the City*. London: Chatto & Windus.

Willin, P. (1977) *Learning to Labour*. Farnborough: Saxon House.

Wilson, E. (1997) Saint Diana, *New Left Review*, 226(November/December): 136–45.

Witz, A. (2001) George Simmel and the Masculinity of Modernity, *Journal of Classical Sociology*, 1(3): 353–70.

Wolf, J. (2000) the feminine in modern art: Benjamin Simmel and the gender of modernity, *Theory, Culture and Society*, 17(6): 33–53.

Wollstonecraft, M. ([1792] 1970) *A Vindication of the Rights of Women*. London: Dent.

Woolf, V. (1928) *Orlando*. London: Hogarth Press.

Woolf, V. ([1929] 1992) *A Room of One's Own*. Oxford: Oxford University Press.

Woolf, V. (1993) *The Crowded Dance of Modern Life*. London: Penguin.

Woolf, V. ([1938] 1992) *Three Guineas*. Oxford: Oxford University Press.

Wouters, C. (1998) Sex and love since the 1960's sexual revolution, *Theory, Culture and Society*, 15(3–4): 187–214.

INDEX

Abbott, Pamela, 16
academic curriculum
    absence of women, 11
    effect on social theory, 23
academic feminism, 7, 8, 11, 12, 91–2,
        99
    deconstruction of gender, 56–7
    gender differentiation, 47
    influence on unpaid work, 32
    involvement in practical issues, 12
    re-readings of Marx, 28–9, 32–3
    sociology, 70, 77, 93–4
    see also feminism; first wave
        feminism; French feminism;
        Marxist feminism; second wave
        feminism
academic world
    attitude to fiction, 35
    discussion of women, 13
    dominance of men, 11, 25
    and social change, 13
achievement, of women in education,
    see examination success
adolescents, peer pressure, gender
        roles and sexual behaviour,
        80
All That is Solid Melts into Air, 4
Althusser, Louis, 32
*An Introduction to Sociology: Feminist
    Perspectives*, 16

androgyny, 45, 68, 106
    see also gender de-differentiation
Armstrong, Nancy, 23–4
'audit culture', 53
Austen, Jane, 18, 36

Babbitt, 39–40
Bad Blood, 103
Barrett, Michele, 4, 48
Baumann, Zygmunt, 26, 71, 72
Beer, Gillian, 25
The Bell Jar, 9, 14
Belsey, Catherine, 28
benefits, 32
    exclusion of women, 82–4
Bentham, Jeremy, 24
Berman, Marshall, 4
Beveridge Report, 56, 83, 102
Beynon, Huw, 39
biological differences, impact, 57
Bloomsbury Group, 74
Bodies that Matter, 58
Bordo, Susan, 88
Bourdieu, Pierre, 33
Bradbury, Malcolm, 93
Brake, Mike, 59
Brassed Off (film), 34
*Breaking Out: Feminist Consciousness
    and Feminist Research*, 50
Bronte, Charlotte, 36

ECONOMY, CULTURE AND SOCIETY
A SOCIOLOGICAL CRITIQUE OF NEO-LIBERALISM

Barry Smart

> ... excellent ... a probing survey of classical and contemporary social theory ... extremely well written and organized ... one of the best overviews of contemporary economy, culture and society I have read.
>
> Professor Douglas Kellner, UCLA

> ... an authoritative analysis and a definitive defence of sociology as a critical theory of the market, politics and social institutions. A balanced and thorough critique of the neo-liberal revolution.
>
> Professor Bryan Turner, University of Cambridge

- How have economic processes and transformations been addressed within classical and contemporary social thought?

- What impact have the market system and market forces had on social life?

- How has the imbalance between the public and private sectors been felt in contemporary society?

Economic factors and processes are at the heart of contemporary social and cultural life and this book is designed to refocus social theorizing to reflect that fact. The author re-interprets the work of classical theorists and, in the context of the move towards social regulation and protection in the 19th and early 20th centuries, he discusses more recent transformations in capitalist economic life that have led to greater flexibility, forms of disorganization, and a neo-liberal regeneration of the market economy. As our lives have become subject to a process of commodification, market forces have assumed an increasing prominence, and the imbalance in resources between private and public sectors has been aggravated. This illuminating text addresses these central concerns, drawing on the work of key social and economic thinkers.

Contents

c.192pp   0 335 20910 6 (Paperback)   0 335 20911 4 (Hardback)

GENERATIONS, CULTURE AND SOCIETY
June Edmunds and Bryan S. Turner

... the most important statement since Mannheim's classic work. It establishes a traumatic events theory of generations, and elaborates a model of generational conflict . . . All this is demonstrated through illuminating analyses . . . For Edmunds and Turner, generations rather than classes have shaped much of the 20th century and beyond.

Professor Randall Collins, University of Pennsylvania

... clearly establishes the relevance of generations as a key sociological concept for understanding cultural change today . . . an excellent book that offers students and academics a lively and up-to-date text on the role and significance of generations, with comprehensive coverage of social scientific debates.

Gerard Delanty, Professor of Sociology, University of Liverpool

- What is the role of generations in social, cultural and political change?
- How is generational consciousness formed?
- What is the significance of inter- and intra-generational conflict and continuity?

Despite the importance of the concept of generations in common sense or lay understanding of cultural change, the study of generations has not played a large part in the development of sociological theory. However, recent social developments, combined with the erosion of a strong class theory, mean that generations need to be reconsidered in relation to cultural change and politics. Moving beyond Karl Mannheim's classical contribution to generations, this book offers a theoretically innovative way of examining the role of generational consciousness in social, cultural and political change through a range of empirical illustrations. On the grounds that existing research on generations has neglected international generational divisions, the book also looks at the interactions between generations and other social categories, including gender and ethnicity, exploring both intra-generational conflict and continuity and considering the circumstances under which generational consciousness may become more salient. The result is a key text for undergraduate courses in social theory, cultural studies and social history, and an essential reference for researchers across these areas, as well as gender, race and ethnicity.

Contents

160pp   0 335 20851 7 (Paperback)   0 335 20852 5 (Hardback)

MAKING SENSE OF SOCIAL MOVEMENTS

Nick Crossley

> ... effectively demonstrates the enduring importance of 'classical' social movement theory ... and provides a cutting edge critical review of recent theoretical developments. This is one of the most important general theoretical texts on social movements for some years.
>
> Paul Bagguley, University of Leeds

- Why and how do social movements emerge?
- In which ways are social movements analysed?
- Can our understanding be enhanced by new perspectives?

Making Sense of Social Movements offers a clear and comprehensive overview of the key sociological approaches to the study of social movements. The author argues that each of these approaches makes an important contribution to our understanding of social movements but that none is adequate on its own. In response he argues for a new approach which draws together key insights within the solid foundations of Pierre Bourdieu's social theory of practice. This new approach transcends the barriers which still often divide European and North American perspectives of social movements, and also those which divide recent approaches from the older 'collective behaviour' approach. The result is a theoretical framework which is uniquely equipped for the demands of modern social movement analysis. The clear and concise style of the text, as well as its neat summaries of key concepts and approaches, will make this book invaluable for undergraduate courses. It will also be an essential reference for researchers.

Contents
Introduction – Social unrest, movement culture and identity: the symbolic interactionists – Smelser's value-added approach – Rational actor theory – Resources, networks and organizations – Opportunities, cognition and biography – Repertoires, frames and cycles – New social movements – Social movements and the theory of practice: a new synthesis – References – Index.

c.192pp   0 335 20602 6 (Paperback)   0 335 20603 4 (Hardback)

FEMINISM

Jane Freedman

- What is the relevance of feminist thought to today's society?
- What do feminists mean by equality and difference?
- Can we find unity in feminist thought, or only conflict?

Feminism provides an introduction to some of the major debates within feminist theory and action. Focusing on the perennial question of equality and difference, the book examines the ways in which this has been played out in different areas of feminist social and political theory. Jane Freedman adopts a refreshing approach by focusing on issues rather than schools of thought. Among the subjects she examines are politics and women's citizenship, paid and unpaid employment and the global economy, sexuality and power, and race and ethnicity. Finally, the book analyses the problem of essentialism for feminism and the challenge of postmodern and poststructuralist theories. Written in a jargon-free style, this book presents a clear and concise introduction to a wide range of feminist thought.

Contents

Introduction: Feminism or feminisms? – Equal or different? The perennial feminist problematic – Feminism and the political: the fight for women's citizenship – Employment and the global economy – Sexuality and power – Ethnicity and identity: the problem of essentialism and the postmodern challenge – Bibliography – Index.

112pp   0 335 20415 5 (Paperback)   0 335 20416 3 (Hardback)

RISK

Roy Boyne

- Is risk always measurable?

- Why are some risks more important?

- Do we take a lot more risks now?

- On whom can we rely for advice?

- How critical is the sociology of risk for understanding contemporary society?

The term 'risk' occurs throughout contemporary social analysis and political commentary. It is now virtually a legal requirement that large organizations throughout the world establish formal risk assessment and risk management procedures. Increasingly dense communication and media networks alert huge numbers of people and organizations to a widening range of threats and possibilities. A basic understanding of the risks themselves may require specific technical knowledge of basic chemistry, or the psychology of motivation, or of contrasting interpretations of injustices deep within the past. However, at the same time as attending to specific risks, there are general questions such as those above which invite reflection.

This wide-ranging and concisely written text is devoted to these general questions, exploring issues such as the measurement of risk in its social context, the idea that the mass media or the political opposition always exaggerate risk, and the notion that the advice of the expert is the best we can get as far as risks are concerned. It asks if there are more risks now and whether a certain level of risk is inevitable or even desirable, and considers for example whether interference with nature has led us to a world which is just too full of risks. Each chapter in the book builds towards a basic picture of risk in the contemporary world, and of the place of the concept of risk within the social sciences today.

Contents
Acknowledgements – The limits of calculation – Risk in the media – Cultural variation or cultural rapture? – Risk-taking – Expert cultures – Risk society? – References – Index.

c.160pp   0 335 20829 0 (Paperback)   0 335 20830 4 (Hardback)